# Farm and Factory: Revolution in the Borders

*John Dent and Rory McDonald*

**Scottish Borders Council**
Economic Development and Environmental Planning

*Farm and Factory: Revolution in the Borders*

© Scottish Borders Council
Council Headquarters
Newtown St. Boswells
MELROSE
Scottish Borders
TD6 0SA

*All rights reserved. No part of this publication may be reproduced, stored in a retrieval system, or transmitted by any means: electronic, electrostatic, magnetic tape, photocopying, recording or otherwise, without prior permission in writing from Scottish Borders Council, nor otherwise be circulated in any form of binding or cover other than that in which is it published and without a similar condition including this condition being imposed on the subsequent user.*

A British Library Cataloguing-in-Publication Data record for this book is available from the British Library

ISBN: 0 9530438 3 5

Designed by the Graphics Section
Scottish Borders Council
Printed and bound by Kelso Graphics, The Knowes, Kelso, Scotland, TD5 7BH

First Published 2001
Economic Development and Environmental Planning, Scottish Borders Council

# Foreword

This is the fourth valuable book produced in recent years by Messrs Dent and McDonald extolling different aspect of the heritage of the Borders. It is important that we should all appreciate the history of the area in which we live, and this volume concentrates on the developing way of life of both rural and urban communities.

I thought that after 32 years as local MP and author of one book and many articles on the Borders, I could claim a reasonable knowledge, but this work produces fascinating glimpses of new enlightenment. The authors refer to the sudden expansion of workers' houses in the late 18th to early 19th centuries in Galashiels and Hawick, describing them as "well-built but cramped", and developed by mill owners. Such was their legacy that a government report in 1959 cited Galashiels as the town in Scotland with the highest percentage of homes without indoor facilities. Government and local government action has since changed that unhealthy picture, but I still recall in the late sixties visiting attractive stone houses with communal outdoor lavatories in their back greens.

On an allied topic, I discovered, for the first time, the tale of the workers' action in one mill in 1900 in "refusing to urinate in the receptacles provided, thus depriving the scouring departing of its principal supply of ammonia".

On transport we learn that the only light railway constructed in the Borders (prior to their demise through invention of the motor car and bus) was from Fountainhall to Lauder, and it was news to me that a canal was proposed but never implemented between Berwick and Ancrum, as also was the fact that Ashiestiel Bridge near Caddonfoot at 40 metres long was in its day the longest single-span rubble-arched bridge in the world. Walkerburn simply did not exist at all until as recently as 1854.

This volume is full of gems of information such as this and including details of changing patterns of agriculture presents a wonderfully rich picture of the life of our forbears in this region of Scotland.

*The Rt. Hon. Lord Steel of Aikwood KBE, PC, DL*

## Acknowledgements

*This book was written, compiled and edited by John Dent and Rory McDonald of the Archaeology and Countryside Section, and designed by the Graphics Section of Scottish Borders Council, as part of the "Heritage Interpretation Project".*

Scottish Borders Council is pleased to acknowledge financial support from the European Regional Development Fund and Scottish Natural Heritage, which assisted in the production of this book.

We would like to thank the following people for their help and advice during the preparation of this book: Richard Allan, Chris Badenoch, Mike Baker, Ian Brown, Louise Comrie, Richard Fawcett, Steve Hunt, Marion Oates, Keith Robeson and the staff of Peebles Tourist Information Centre.

*Farm and Factory: Revolution in the Borders*

## *Introduction*

For many visitors, the landscape of the Scottish Borders comes as a total surprise after the bleak moors and hills that they have crossed to get here. Apart from the approaches from Northumberland, which cross the lower Tweed, most roads into the region rise over hills either at the boundary, or soon afterwards. Once inside, the roads follow valleys that widen out into arable farmland punctuated with trees and tracts of woodland. Ancient volcanic hills ensure that this landscape is never bland, and few parts of Britain provide such variety. Most of the tumbling streams and rivers ultimately flow into the Tweed, renowned for its salmon, and out into the North Sea. The quality of the landscape is complemented by the quality of the air, the cleanliness of which is reflected in the growth of lichens on many trees.

The underlying structure of this landscape is ancient, but the surface dressing of trees, hedges, fields, pastures and buildings is largely the product of the last three centuries. During this period social and economic changes have created parks, woods and forests where few trees grew before and cultivated fields on former bogs and marshes. Some ploughlands and villages have disappeared into sheepwalks, and rustic tracks have been turned into metalled highways; the railway has come and gone and villages have grown into industrial towns dominated by textile mills, originally driven by the water of the Border rivers.

Scottish Borders has a remarkable history, which reflects the changing relationship between Scotland and England over the centuries since they came into being. In the 12$^{th}$ century the social structure was developed that gave communities an interest in their own affairs and sparked off rivalry, particularly in trade, between neighbouring towns. Scarcely had the region acquired a degree of prosperity when three centuries of Anglo-Scottish wars intervened to impose long-lasting and crushing setbacks on the whole region. Only from the 17$^{th}$ century did lasting peace provide the basis for enduring agricultural development and commercial progress which grew from that.

Experiments in farming methods, development of labour-saving devices, cultivation of new land and re-organisation of the traditional fields enabled farmers to produce a surplus of food. From the mid-18$^{th}$ century improvements to the road network helped this surplus to reach the market towns and support a growing urban population. The first water-powered textile mill opened at Innerleithen in 1788 and marked the start of the development of the textile towns of the Borders. Cottage industry declined as manufacturing became concentrated in urban workshops, which supplied markets throughout the expanding British Empire. With commercial prosperity came all the trappings of the Victorian era, including many buildings that have endured subsequent periods of retrenchment and now form part of the region's heritage.

The purpose of this book is to guide the reader around the landscape and buildings of the Borders and explain the part they played in a revolution that transformed the whole of Britain. This process was not confined to one town or one part of the region, nor was it a political event; it was a period of swift economic and social change, and was felt in farms and factories across the land.

# Farm and Factory: Revolution in the Borders

Please note, however, that mention of an archaeologically important site in the text does not indicate that it may be visited. The reader should be aware that although many sites are marked on Ordnance Survey maps or may be readily visible in the landscape, most are located on private land and are not generally accessible. At the end of the book the reader will find a list of those sites which are open to the public at the time of printing, those museums which contain collections of artefacts, and sources of further information.

**Please remember, whenever visiting these sites, always follow the Country Code:**

- Guard against all risk of fire
- Fasten all gates
- Keep dogs under close control
- Keep to paths across farmland
- Avoid damaging fences
- Leave no litter
- Safeguard water supplies
- Protect wildlife, wild plants and trees
- Go carefully on country roads
- Respect the life of the countryside

## Table of Contents

| | |
|---|---|
| **Foreword** | 3 |
| **Acknowledgements** | 4 |
| **Introduction** | 5 |
| **Part 1: The historical background** | 9 |
| Agricultural Change | 13 |
| Industrial Advances | 17 |
| **Part 2: Way of Life** | 23 |
| Levels of Society | 24 |
| Food and drink | 33 |
| Communications | 36 |
| **Part 3: Effect upon the landscape** | 45 |
| Expansion and reorganisation of farmland | 46 |
| Raw materials and energy | 52 |
| **Part 4: Surviving archaeological features** | 57 |
| Transport remains | 58 |
| Agricultural remains | 63 |
| Industrial remains | 69 |
| **Further Reading** | 76 |
| **Glossary** | 78 |
| **Sites to Visit** | 81 |
| **Index** | 87 |

# Farm and Factory: Revolution in the Borders

# Part 1:

# The Historical Background

# Farm and Factory: Revolution in the Borders

| Chronology | Events in the Borders | The Wider Picture |
|---|---|---|
| 17th century | 1603 Union of the Crowns created the conditions for lasting peace on the Borders. | Increasing interest in agriculture; experiments with root crops and rotational systems. |
| 18th century | Borderers such as James Dickson return from oversees and invest in local developments. | 1707 Act of Union provides access to English oversees trade and colonies. |
| | 1729 Duke of Argyll drains marshland to create The Whim estate.<br><br>1740s onwards Enclosure of open fields<br>1740s Potatoes and Turnips first cultivated in Berwickshire | Land reclamation and enclosure. Traditional rural social fabric dismantled Agricultural experiments include widespread sheep farming in uplands. Displaced and landless classes seek work in towns. |
| | 1750s first Turnpike Trusts established in the Borders. Main urban centres connected by 1770. | 1751 Turnpike Act leads to better roads and improved trade. |
| | 1737 Andrew Roger of Cavers invents Scotland's first winnowing machine.<br><br>1760s John Small invents a new plough. | Technological improvements in agriculture and manufacturing. Water Frame (1768); Stream Engine (1769); Spinning Jenny (1774); Mule (1779); Meikle's Threshing Machine (1787) |
| | 1747 New harbour works started at Eyemouth.<br><br>1760 New villages of Gavinton (1760), Carlops (1784) and Newcastleton (1793) built for weavers.<br><br>1777 Manufacturers' Corporation established in Galashiels<br><br>1788 First modern factory in the Borders opened at Caerlee Mill, Innerleithen | Investment in industry develops with capital from agriculture and trade. specialised centres established. |

*Fig.1* Events relating to the Agricultural and Industrial Revolutions.

## Farm and Factory: Revolution in the Borders

| Chronology | Events in the Borders | The Wider Picture |
|---|---|---|
| 19th century | Commercial growth reflecting national trends. | Development of world-wide commercial empire founded on British manufacturing. Social issues develop with changing circumstances. |
| | 1803 Kelso Bridge opened.<br><br>1820 Union Suspension Bridge opened.<br><br>1846 Edinburgh to Berwick railway opened; network develops in Borders over following 20 years | Transport continues to improve using innovative technology and design.<br><br>Railways develop from mining industry. Countrywide network created by later 19th century.<br><br>Britain reaches industrial peak 1850s. |
| | 1820s Gas lighting used at Abbotsford, Bowhill and other country houses. Duns and Peebles Gas Companies founded. | Practical adoption of scientific discoveries, such as steam engine and electric telegraph. 1880 first electric light used in Britain at Cragside, Northumberland. |
| | 1832 Cholera outbreak affects Hawick and Kelso.<br><br>1881 Eyemouth Fishing Disaster.<br><br>1891 Borders population peaks at 128,261. | Rapid population growth. Public health and order concerns lead to Police Acts which encourage urban improvements. Growth of charitable trusts for poor relief. |
| 20th century | Position in world textile market affected by developing competitors. | Inability to maintain commercial and industrial pre-eminence. Loss of empire. |
| | 1969 Last railway stations close with Waverley Route.<br><br>Late 20th century. Decline in manufacturing. | Internal combustion engine gradually comes to dominate transport. Increased competition from abroad. Decline of rail system. Industrial contraction. |

# Farm and Factory: Revolution in the Borders

## Part 1: The Historical Background

The geography of the Borders area has heavily influenced the ability of the surrounding countryside to support populations of varying size. Villages, many founded more than 1,000 years ago, are characteristic of the primarily arable farming areas of the Merse, Teviotdale and the lower Tweed, whereas the population of the upland grazing areas is distributed among isolated farms and dispersed hamlets or *touns* (**fig.2**).

In the 12th century King David I incorporated these communities into his machinery of government by the creation of ecclesiastical parishes to serve their spiritual needs and by the allocation of civil manors to Norman landlords from estates that he held in England. The Border shires he governed through the county towns, which he established as Royal Burghs. These settlements, such as Jedburgh and Peebles, had trading privileges and town councils. He sponsored the establishment of monasteries with self-sustaining estates and these developed farming on an unprecedented scale, with particular emphasis on wool production for the continental market.

Although monasteries played a key role in agricultural developments of the Later Middle Ages, the Border abbeys suffered particularly

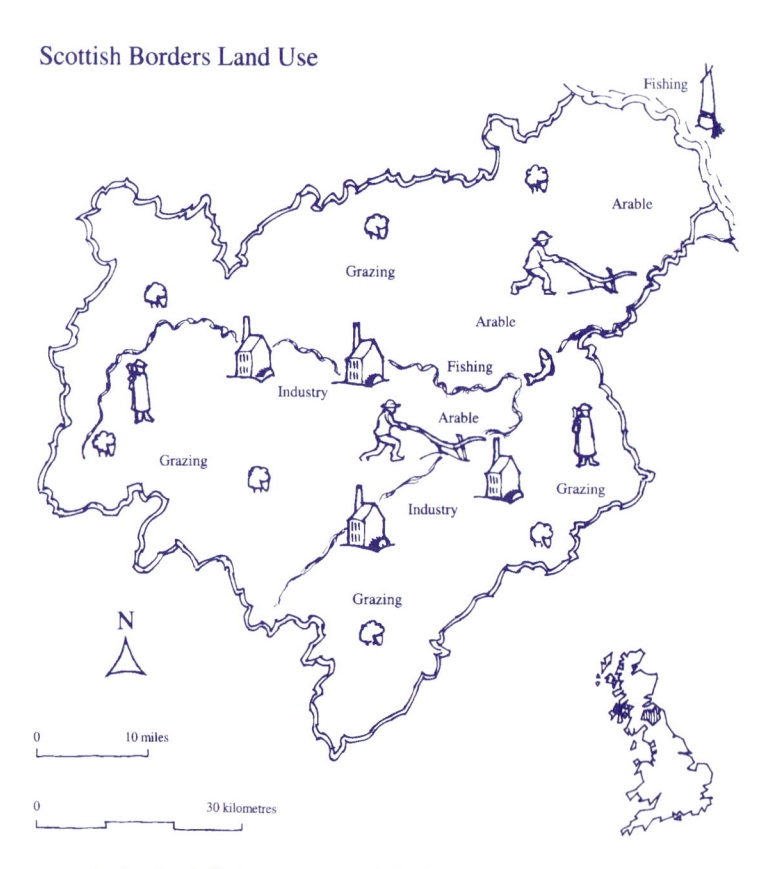

***Fig.2*** *For centuries the Border hills have supported flocks of cattle and sheep, whereas arable farming has prospered in the central and eastern lowlands. Industry developed along the river valleys where water could be harnessed to power mills. Fish, caught in the rivers or netted in the North Sea, have been an important source of food since prehistoric times.*

badly in the Wars of Independence and the centuries of unrest and open warfare that followed (*see Christian Heritage in the Borders and Warfare and Fortifications in the Borders*). Trade diminished too, following the loss of Berwick to England in 1482 and the decline and abandonment of Old Roxburgh (Kelso) in the 16$^{th}$ century. By the 1560s the Borders had lost its two most important centres for the import and export of goods as well as its most powerful farming interests – the Border abbeys – which closed as a consequence of the *Reformation*.

Although these events were an obstacle to the development of trade and agriculture, other processes helped to prepare the ground for future economic improvements. The *Renaissance* brought printing to Scotland and made classical texts, hitherto preserved as manuscripts in monastic libraries, available to a wider audience. Writings such as *Cato's de Agricultura* generated interest in the science of farming among a growing middle class with capital to invest in agricultural experiments.

## Agricultural Change

### *Traditional rural communities*

Before landowners began to "improve" the land the type of agriculture which was practised had remained unaltered for hundreds of years. Open fields made up of cultivated ridges surrounded settlements, whether they were villages of the more fertile lowland areas or the small irregular hamlets of the hill country.

In the uplands *ferm* touns were hamlets which focused on a single farm, although the farmland was often worked by a number of joint tenants. When the parish church provided the focus for a hamlet, such settlements were known as *kirk* touns, an example of which is Kirkton Manor (Manor) near Peebles. Immediately around the toun was a common *infield*, which was intensively cultivated as individually worked strips. Beyond this common field was an *outfield* for summer grazing that also saw the occasional production of a crop of oats. Uncultivated land included wooded and wetland areas, such as bogs and *lochans*, and areas which were more suitable for grazing than ploughing. The only drains were the hollows between the rigs, where stones and weeds were also thrown. Ferm touns rarely grew into villages, but instead produced satellite hamlets that sometimes shared part of the same name, such as Easter and Wester Mountbenger (Yarrow).

Other types of settlements included *shielings* and forest *steads*. Shielings were temporary shelters used by herdsmen during the summer months in areas of high pasture. Place names such as Galashiels and Lambertonshiels (Mordington) point to the former existence of these structures, although the shielings themselves have vanished long ago, or have grown into permanent settlements as the boundaries of agriculture expanded. Forest steads were farms of various sizes in royal hunting preserves and numerous examples existed in the Ettrick and Yarrow valleys such as Sundhope (Yarrow) and Old Kirkhope (Ettrick). The emphasis in such places was on animal husbandry and medieval rents were levied in cattle and lambs.

### *Clearances*

The remains of many former ferm and kirk touns survive in the Border countryside and are proof that communities are not permanent. The centuries of warfare which affected the Borders led to the abandonment of some settlements, but many of the villages affected by the Earl of Hertford's devastating raid of 1545, which were afterwards described as "*brent, rased or cast downe,*" re-emerged and still exist in some form today. The earliest detailed maps of the region show many settlements that are now much reduced in size or have disappeared altogether. These maps post-date the Anglo-Scottish wars, and alterations in the settlements shown on them cannot be linked to warfare, but must be due to other factors.

The most likely reason for this movement of people from the countryside is the need to make a living in the absence of work at home. Population growth may account for part of this, particularly after c.1770, but the main reason for the removal of much of the rural population is that landlords introduced farming methods and machinery that needed fewer agricultural workers.

As the agricultural potential of much of the land in the Borders was extremely limited, increasingly large tracts of land were devoted to the rearing of livestock. Wool was a leading export in the medieval Borders economy and the abbeys ran large swathes of the region as highly intensive sheep ranches. These required only a small number of shepherds to watch over vast flocks, often at the expense of local farming communities who had previously grown crops on the same land. Concentration on livestock may also have been influenced by the frequent threat of warfare and by the actions of *reivers*, who were even active during periods of uneasy peace. Grain and other crops presented difficulties when it came to carrying them off and so would normally be destroyed in warfare or raids. Cattle and sheep were mobile and were a more dependable source of wealth and food, for they could be hidden from raiders, recovered from rustling parties, or even brought into the region by reiving Borderers.

## *Improvement and Enclosure*

The shared use of the unenclosed common field was a consistent obstacle to any individual attempts to experiment in crop husbandry. Any single open field would normally have the same crop sown on all the ridges by all the tenants, since any individual variation would impact on the rest. A strip left fallow or sown with grass would infect neighbouring holdings. Normally the single crop ripened and was harvested at the same time across the whole common field, then the animals were let onto the ground to graze the stubble and manure the field for the next season. The animals would spoil any additional variety of crop that was not ready for harvest. As long as the fields were unenclosed and worked in common, opportunities for experiment were extremely restricted.

In the 17th century landowners such as Sir Alexander Cockburn, who had estates at Langton and Simprim (Swinton), introduced a system from England whereby land, following a cereal crop, was allowed to remain under grass for several seasons for the soil to recover, after which cereals were grown once more. Where the distribution of holdings allowed, this practice could operate within the common field system and had the advantage of increased yields. The result was that during the later 17th century the lowlands of Scotland were able to produce enough food to feed the population even during periods of crop failure.

The pace of improvement accelerated in the 18th century, especially after the Union of 1707, which gave Scotland access to the British Empire and, in particular, to increased contact with England. This led, not only to the spread of ideas, but to a growing appreciation amongst the land-owning classes of the backwardness of agriculture on their estates compared to those south of the Border. A few of these landowners began to improve their estates in the early years of this century; John Swinton of Swinton, for example, is recorded as having drained, *marled*, and completely enclosed his whole estate. In 1729 the third Duke of Argyll started work on The Whim (Newlands), a country estate which he created by draining and planting an area of barren moorland. A shortage of capital was a major obstacle to investment and experiment in this period, but as the century progressed landowners took the opportunity increasingly to drain, enclose and plant their lands. Such improvements radically changed the Borders from an open, virtually treeless landscape to an expanse of enclosed field systems, drained and bounded by hawthorn hedges or stone walls.

Linked to the overall improvement of the

farming landscape was the development of animals and crops. Cattle were fattened in the newly laid out parks and English breeds were imported to improve the quality of the livestock. New crop varieties were introduced and grown in rotation for the first time. It is unclear when some of these varieties made their first appearance. Potatoes are credited to Lord Stair in 1724, but were not grown as a field crop until later: in 1740 at Chirnside or 1747 Cothill (Polwarth). Similarly, it is unclear as to whether it was John Cockburn of Ormiston who introduced turnips in 1725 or Lord Kames on his Berwickshire estate in 1746. Dr John Rutherford of Melrose fattened his bullocks with turnips in 1747 with such outstanding success that people refused to eat the huge beasts.

Midlem (Bowden) is a village that still retains much of its traditional plan, with the shape of its open fields preserved on each side (**Plate 1**). Properties in the village still had associated strips of common field land in the mid-20$^{th}$ century. Such fields were divided into individual rigs, groups of which formed a single farming unit. These blocks were shared out among the farming community and a degree of fairness meant that good, bad and indifferent land was shared evenly. Few, if any, farmers had all their land blocked together, and this placed limitations on their ability to work any new ground that was opened up through drainage and reclamation of moorland. One effect of the improvement was to reduce the centralising effect of village communities by dispersing farmers to detached homesteads.

If circumstances were favourable, a farmer might be able to enclose the strips which made up his holding. This might come about through inheritance, purchase, or exchange and such fields can sometimes be recognised from their distinctive shape among the more square fields of subsequent enclosure. Such fields may date from the late 17$^{th}$ or early 18$^{th}$ century and examples can still be seen, for instance at Lilliesleaf.

Enclosure of the whole common field system involved all concerned and required the services of a surveyor. In England only an Act of Parliament could accomplish such enclosure, but in Scotland the lands were usually held under *feudal* tenure of the *laird*, who was normally the driving force behind the process. The total arable land was surveyed and divided into squared fields, which were then allocated proportionately to the farming community. This process could not accommodate all the former landholders, and many people lost what little land they had. The social effects of this were divisive and long lasting.

Where a farm holding was too small to be viable under the commercial regime a proprietor simply waited until the lease was due and then refused to renew it. On the one hand former farmers now found themselves reliant on an employer for their livelihood, while on the other the beneficiaries of this system found themselves employing erstwhile fellow farmers to work their expanded holdings. In Berwickshire the mixed arable and livestock farms were among the largest lowland farms in Scotland, often running to hundreds of hectares.

Although most of the enclosures took place in the second half of the 18$^{th}$ century some occurred earlier. As early as 1632, Robert Ker, the earl of Ancrum was planning improvements to his estate. However, in general, the initial improvements began in the 1740s and continued until the early 1770s, at which point there was a period of poor harvests due to a series of bad summers and the process slowed so that only the very wealthy could continue to develop their estates. Towards the end of the 1780s the climate improved once more and the process started again. The 18$^{th}$ century was also a period that saw the development of large estates such as those at Mellerstain (Earlston), Bowhill (Selkirk) and Floors (Kelso). Each of these focused on a large country house amid a designed landscape (**Plate 2**).

The amount of available agricultural land was

# Farm and Factory: Revolution in the Borders

further increased with large-scale reclamation of areas of marshland through drainage. Vast tracts of long established wetlands disappeared although place names such as the Billie Mire (Chirnside/Coldingham) and Cowbog (Morebattle), recall their existence. Other marshland areas such as Yetholm Loch and Greenlaw Moss were greatly reduced at the same time. Slowly and incrementally the countryside of the Borders was transformed to produce a patchwork of enclosed land and improved fields with older field systems still in existence in areas thought to be too poor to cultivate.

The full potential of the land could not have been realised without labour saving devices and the ingenuity of inventors was directed at these. In 1737, Andrew Roger, a farmer at Cavers invented the country's first *winnowing* machine. Although this appliance quickly found favour amongst his fellow farmers, the Secession Church was outraged, declaring it impious to interfere with the natural course or volume of the wind. In the 1760s James Small of Blackadder Mount (Edrom) revolutionised agriculture in Britain by his development from the Yorkshire plough of a new swing plough that turned the earth much more effectively (**fig.3**). This, and the *Threshing Machine* devised by Andrew Meikle, a millwright from near East Linton (East Lothian: 1787) helped to improve yields and as a result larger surpluses were produced. Machines for speeding up the processing of grain and preparing it for the mill required a driving force. Over much of the Borders the topography favoured the use of waterpower, but where this was not available horsepower was harnessed by means of a *rotary gin* geared to the machinery. The need for a reliable power source for machinery was first registered in agriculture but was soon also recognised in mining, factories and transport.

***Fig.3*** *19th century horse plough that incorporates the shaped mould board developed by James Small in the 1760s.*

## Industrial Advances

The Industrial Revolution was partly a result of the change which had taken place in the agricultural landscape and shared many features with it. As the 18th and 19th centuries progressed the major impact of new developments was increasingly felt in the fields of manufacturing, mining and transport.

Grain mills were the largest early industrial sites and these, and most other devices, were primarily powered by water, although some windmills did exist in the Borders in the 19th century. Water and wind driven mills were initially used to grind grain, however, as both technology and industry developed these power sources were adapted to run machinery for textile production or to operate saw mills. In the 19th century water and wind power were increasingly supplemented or replaced by steam powered engines.

## *Manufacturing*

The traditional basis for commerce in Scotland was the production of goods made by hand at home. Markets where such commodities could be traded were based in the burghs and much of the consumption was local. The Industrial Revolution transformed production, taking it from the cottage to the factory, and massively increasing the output by using powered machines to replace traditional handicrafts.

By the 18th century industries in Scotland and throughout Europe had developed from rural origins where every farming family contained members who could weave wool to make clothes, build tools to use around the farm and perform a variety of other occupations. There was, as yet, very limited technological development and many manufactured goods still arrived as foreign imports. Each town tended to have its specialities; Selkirk was renowned for its shoes, so much so that Bonnie Prince Charlie demanded 2,000 pairs of shoes from the town in 1745 and inhabitants are still known as "Souters" (shoemakers).

The main rural industry was based on wool. However, in the late 18th century the Borders textile industries were still small-scale, cottage-based and scattered among hill farms in many cases, with much of the production taking place during the slack periods in the farming calendar. In an effort to concentrate and encourage weaving some of the more ambitious Borders landowners created planned villages. Of these Gavinton (Langton: 1760) was the first, Newcastleton (Castleton: 1793) was the largest, while developments at Carlops (West Linton: 1784) were on a more modest scale (**Plate 3**).

A Manufacturers' Corporation was established in Galashiels in 1777 and in 1788 Alexander Brodie built the first modern textile factory, equipped with such English machinery as Arkwright's *water frame* and Crompton's *spinning mule*, at Caerlee Mill (Innerleithen: **back cover**). By that time output of manufactured woollen goods had begun to rise significantly and by 1828 the Gala Water was running at capacity, supplying ten mills in Galashiels and obliging manufacturers there to expand into Selkirk (**fig.4**). The industry reached its peak in the 1880s after which it suffered from the imposition of import duties by the United States. Textiles continued to dominate the Borders economy throughout most of the 20th century and have only gone into serious decline in the 1980s and 1990s.

The rise in industrial output and the increased size of many of the farm holdings brought about a shift in living patterns and employment throughout Scotland. Male and female workers were displaced when leases to tenants were not renewed or farms were amalgamated. Often unable to find other agricultural employment, these men and women were forced to move from the countryside and to seek work in the new mills and factories in the rapidly growing towns. Coupled with this was a rise in the birth rate, but more importantly a decline in mortality, particularly amongst infants. This was due, in

# Farm and Factory: Revolution in the Borders

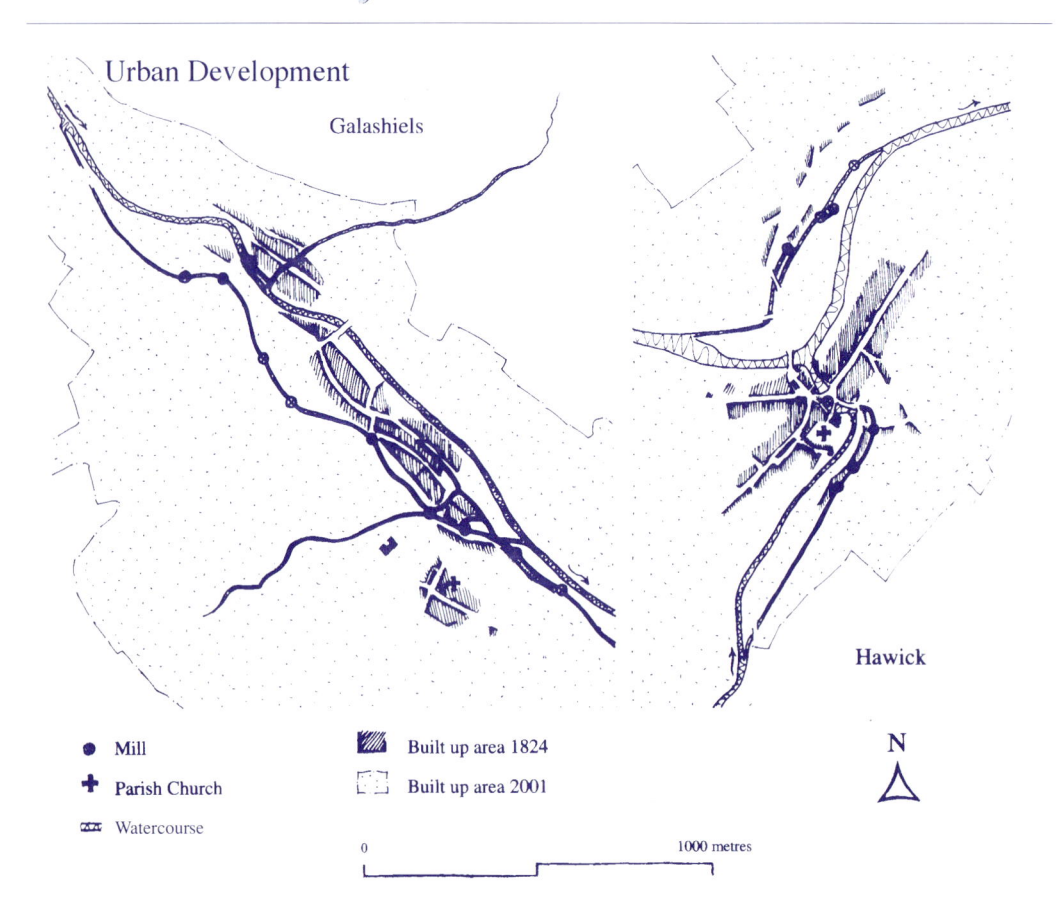

**Fig.4** *Galashiels and Hawick both developed as Burghs of Barony in the 16th century, each with its own Market Place, Parish Church and Corn Mill. From the late 18th century the mill lades also powered woollen mills and new lades were constructed as production expanded. At Galashiels the old town became a backwater and by 1824 the town centre had shifted northwards to its present position. At Hawick the waters of the Teviot and its tributary, the Slitrig, were harnessed to drive textile mills as the town expanded.*

no small way, to the introduction of vaccinations against diseases such as smallpox (1796) and a rise in food production which made death through famine far less common.

In order to accommodate this expanding (and increasingly sedentary) workforce landowners began to provide improved accommodation in planned villages such as Carlops, Newcastleton and Gavinton while the factory owners built rows of terraced houses. The dwellings in the new planned villages were often custom-built to encourage and facilitate the weaving of cloth.

There were also other benefits of this 'building boom'. The need for stone and other materials for housing encouraged other industries such as mining, brick making and quarrying.

## Minerals

The geology of the Borders is poor in minerals, but contains some useful building materials. Medieval and later extraction of lead, silver, copper and perhaps iron, mainly from the West Linton area, was not followed up by more concerted efforts once extractive techniques had improved. However, in the 18th and 19th centuries there was exploitation of coal around West Linton, and open cast extraction is still taking place on Harlaw Muir. Sources of lime, mainly as an *antacid* additive to soils, were exploited in Liddesdale and at West Linton.

The need for building materials to support the growing demand led to the establishment of numerous quarries, particularly exploiting the hard *igneous* rocks which make up the Borders' many volcanic intrusions. Craighouse Quarry (Earlston) is still a valuable source of hard rock for road building. Sand and gravel quarries were exploited, particularly in the river valleys and among the post-glacial deposits at the foot of the Pentland Hills near West Linton. Bricks and tiles were made from clay deposits at a number of sites. The bricks to build the core of Marchmont House (Polwarth: 1750-54) were made for the purpose from clay deposits at Greenlawdean (Greenlaw), while the ruined kiln of a 19th century commercial tileworks can still be seen at Whitrig Bog (Mertoun: **fig.5**).

## *Transport*

The growth of the population, the development of commercial agriculture and the expansion of industry created an increasing demand for a better communications network. An Act of 1669 for Repairing Highways and Bridges introduced

*Fig.5* *This 19th century brick kiln at Mertoun formed part of the "Whitrigbog Tileworks" and was just one site where glacial clay deposits were exploited to produce bricks for developing local industries.*

## Turnpikes in the Borders

- Founded 18th Century
- Founded 19th Century

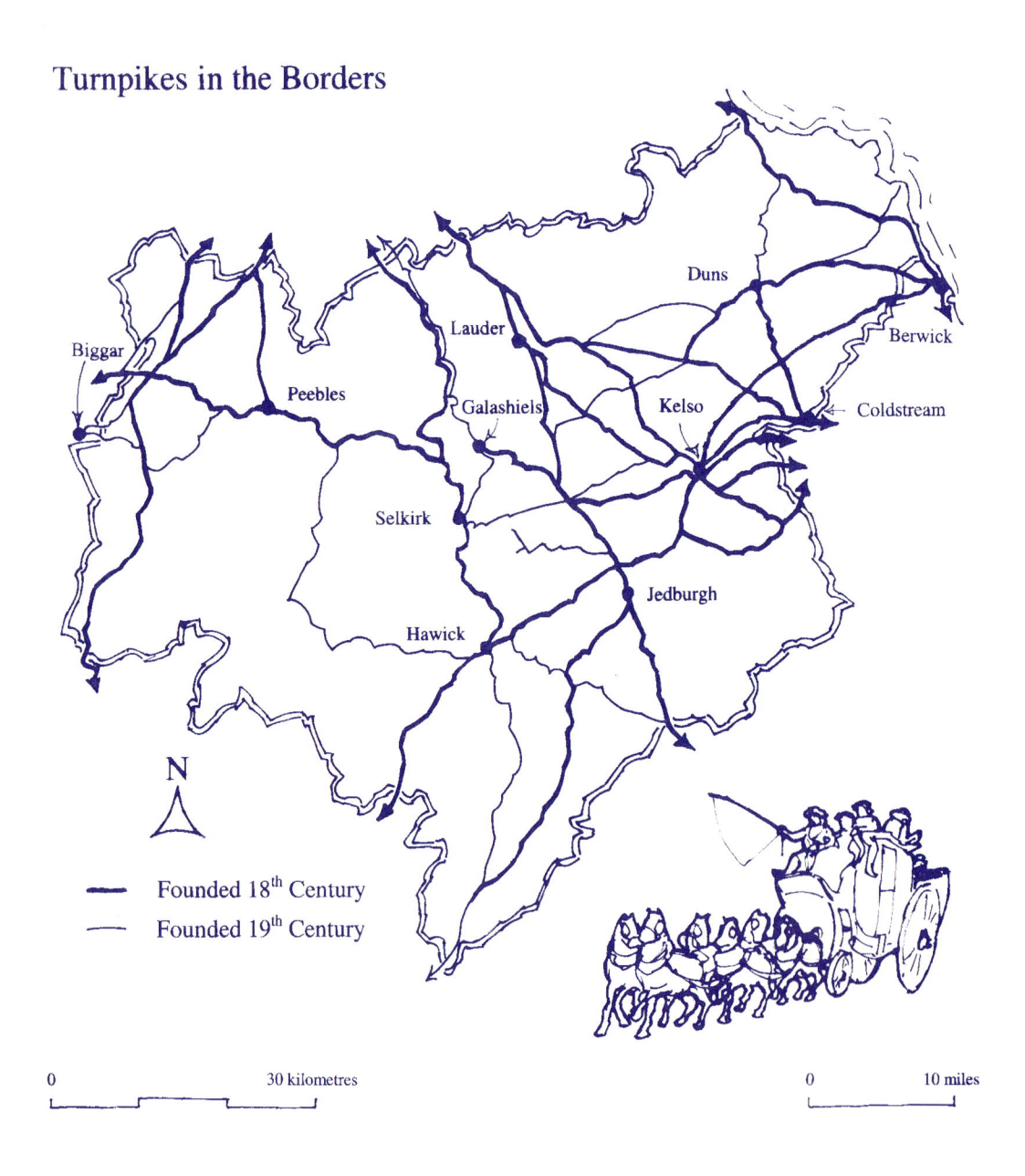

***Fig.6*** *The primitive medieval roads of the Borders were such an obstacle to communication and commerce that from the mid-18th century a series of Turnpike Trusts were established for their improvement. By 1800 all the principal routes had been upgraded and new Trusts attended to secondary roads.*

a compulsory duty to local *heritors* to impress their tenants for six days unpaid labour annually during "parish road days". This burden was later commuted to a money tax to the same ends and, in 1751, an act was passed to enable the establishment of *Turnpike* Trusts in Scotland. These trusts were set up to develop the links between Borders towns and to places beyond (**fig.6**). River crossings provided ample work for builders and particularly prestigious bridges attracted the participation of architect/ engineers such as James Smeaton (Coldstream 1763-66: **Plate 4**), John Rennie (Kelso Bridge 1803) and Capt. Sir Samuel Brown (Union Suspension Bridge 1819-20: Hutton). Much improved stage coach services emerged to take advantage of the new roads and link Borders towns to the capital. The Kelso Flier (1795) was the first regular service which ran between the White Swan Inn, Kelso and MacFarlane's in Edinburgh's Canongate, and took ten hours over the journey.

In 18th century England water proved to be a more effective way of moving large quantities of goods and the country was criss-crossed by canals. The Statistical Account (c.1790) records that a survey had been undertaken with a mind to construct a canal from the coast, inland at least as far as Ancrum Bridge. Although nothing ever came of this project it shows that canal-building fever was also felt in the Borders.

In the first part of the 19th century two of the most prominent engineers of the day, John Macadam and Thomas Telford surveyed roads in the Borders. Telford in particular surveyed the roads leading between Edinburgh and Carlisle and the various routes between Edinburgh and Newcastle. In 1810 Telford surveyed the Tweed Valley for a proposed railway between Glasgow and Berwick. This was designed to take horse-drawn trucks and was never built, but the development of the steam locomotive in the 1820s made railways a reality.

The first railway came to the Borders on its way to link Edinburgh and London via Berwick and Newcastle, and between 1846 and 1901 every town in the Borders was linked into the rail network.

After the capture of Berwick by the English in 1482 and the subsequent incorporation of the town into the Kingdom of England the Borders had no natural harbour. Eyemouth was utilised at that time as a small fishing port by the monks of Coldingham Priory and various inlets, such as Cove (Cockburnspath) and Burnmouth (Ayton) were used as landing sites but none of these had been developed to any great extent. Eyemouth then assumed a greater importance and was, during the course of the 16th century, fortified. This strategic importance continued to be recognised after the creation of the United Kingdom and the port continued to be defended (*see Warfare and Fortifications in the Borders*). It was not, however, until the 18th century that any improvements were undertaken at Eyemouth and Cove in an attempt to improve the fishing industry. The works at Cove proved to be unsuccessful. During the 19th and 20th centuries many improvements were carried out, again at Cove and also at Burnmouth, St Abbs (Coldingham) and Eyemouth. These were beneficial to the fishing industry and even the Great Fishing Disaster at Eyemouth in 1881 could not retard its progress. In the late 20th century further works were undertaken to improve the facilities at Eyemouth to ensure its future well into the 21st century and beyond.

The growth of the British Empire, from the mid-18th century until its climax in the reign of Queen Victoria (1837-1901), enabled many Borderers to travel throughout the globe, taking their expertise with them and learning new techniques as they travelled. Many found prosperity in other parts of the Empire, while others made their fortunes through increased opportunities for trade. Upon their return they bought property and estates and built themselves elegant homes. Some of these residences can still be seen, for example Ednam House Hotel (Kelso: James

# Farm and Factory: Revolution in the Borders

*Fig.7 Ednam House, Kelso was originally known as Havana House. It was designed by James Nisbet for James Dickson, who had left Kelso as a fugitive for the New World and returned in 1760 a wealthy merchant.*

Dickson: **fig.7**), and Harmony Hall (Melrose: Robert Waugh).

The Agricultural Revolution established the basis for development of the industrial economy. It produced a nation confident in its ability to produce more than enough food for its needs and removed the fear of famine. At the same time it provided the capital to invest in industry and the workforce for the new factories. From the late 18th century Britain led the world in commerce until other nations, notably the United States and Germany, caught up in the later 19th century. In the 19th century farming and manufacturing reached their peak outputs. Since then there has been a long decline in both of these sectors of the economy. This change of fortune at the regional level has reflected an overall national trend, which has been exacerbated due to the relatively poor local communications network, especially after rail closures during the 1960s.

# Part 2:

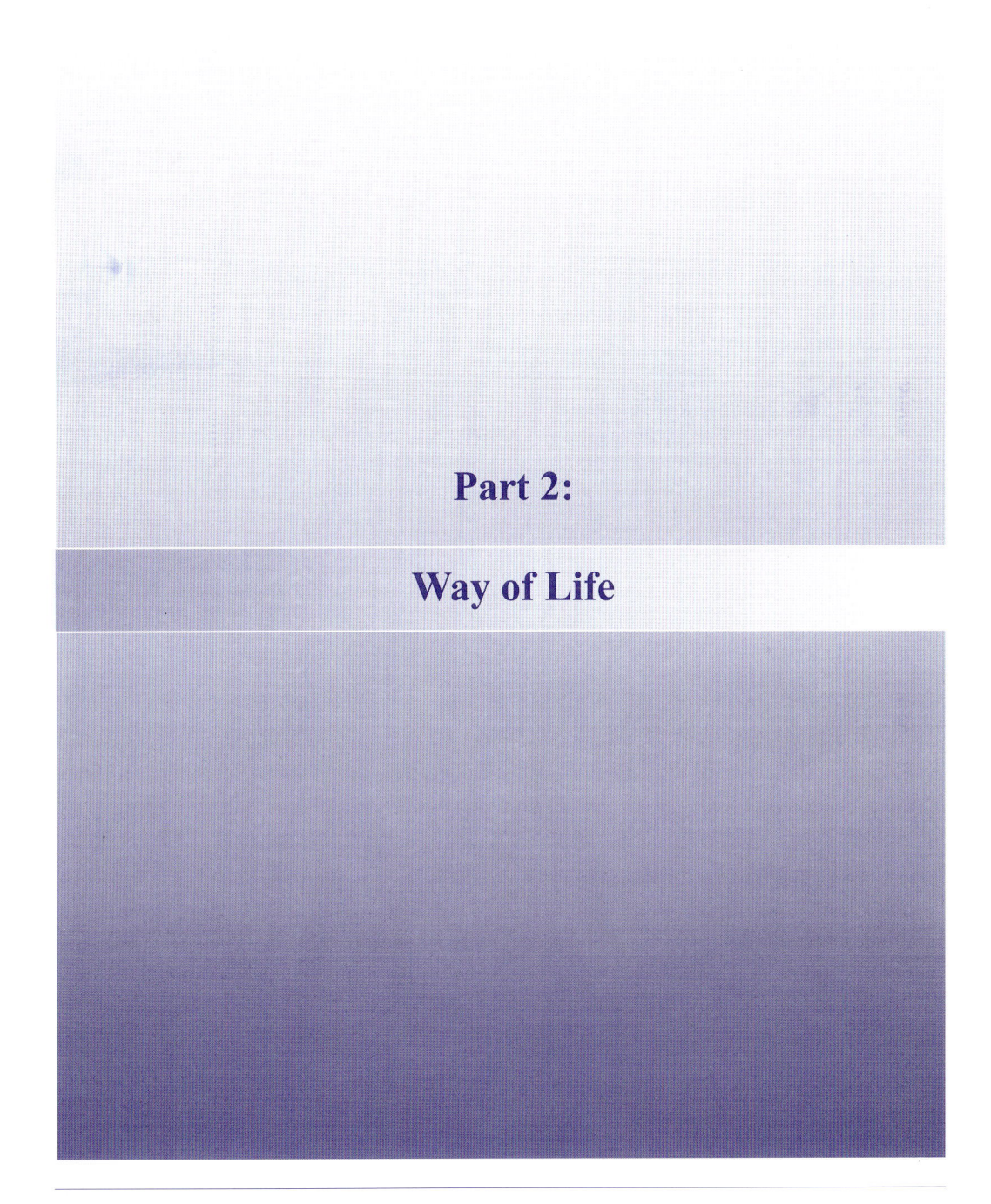

# Way of Life

# Farm and Factory: Revolution in the Borders

## Part 2: Way of Life

The last four centuries have borne witness to a complete change in the size, lifestyle, working and living conditions of the population. In the period discussed within this book there were radical changes to traditional roles in society, brought about by a revolution in agriculture, communications and industry.

## Levels of Society

The Industrial Revolution was the catalyst for population growth throughout Britain. In 1811, when the Industrial Revolution was still in its early years, the population of Britain and Ireland was 18.5 million. This has since trebled to more than 62 million in 2001, an increase of more than 200%. The growth in population of Scotland reflects this trend, rising from 1.8 million in 1811 to 5.1 million in 2001. This rise is due, in the main, to a much healthier population that survived the perils of childhood, or childbirth to live longer, supported by increased job opportunities and a surplus of food.

Although there has been an overall population growth in the Borders, this does not begin to approach the national trend. Dr Alexander Webster's census of 1755 gave the first reliable population figures for the region and indicates that the population of the Border counties of Berwick, Roxburgh, Selkirk and Peebles was 69,225. By 1801 the figure was 75,308 and by 1891 had grown to 128,261, but by 2001 the population of the Borders (which also includes small parts of the former counties of Midlothian and East Lothian) had fallen back to an estimated 106,900 (**fig.8**).

## *The Rural Population*

The bulk of the medieval population of Scotland was rural and this was particularly true in areas such as the Borders. As late as 1690 only 10% to 15% lived in urban settlements, although this had increased to 50% by 1831. This emphasises the fact that prior to the Industrial Revolution even larger settlements such as Hawick or

Population Change in the Borders

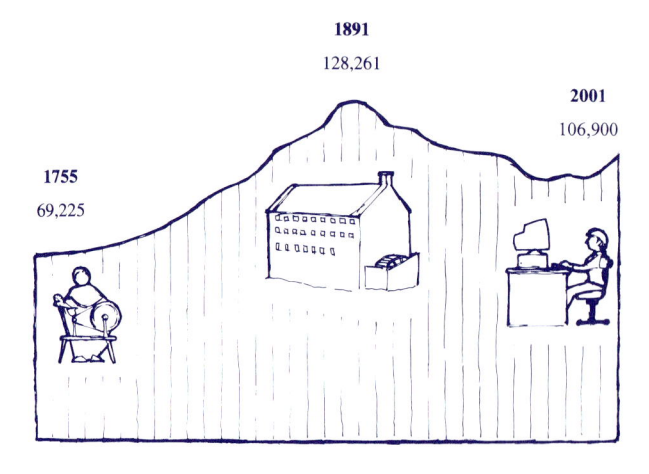

*Fig.8  The population of the Borders had already begun to grow by the time of Webster's Census of 1755. Greater food production and the openings provided by burgeoning industry encouraged further increases, leading to a peak in the late 19th century. Gradual decline in the earlier 20th century was reversed after 1970, partly by migration to the countryside by commuters.*

## Farm and Factory: Revolution in the Borders

Peebles were home to only a few hundred inhabitants. The majority of the population lived in and around farms and these hamlets were often far larger than today.

Since the Middle Ages land in Scotland has continued to change hands by charter with the consent of a feudal superior. In the 18th and 19th centuries the most influential and powerful land-owning group in the Borders countryside consisted of a small number of high-ranking families who owned the majority of the land. Families such as the Homes and the Swintons had held land directly from the Crown since before the Battle of Bannockburn (1314). Other families rose to prominence in the 15th and 16th centuries and in many cases profited from the disposal of monastic property after the Reformation. The fortunes of the Kers of Cessford, for example, rose sharply after 1560 when they acquired much Kelso Abbey property around Selkirk and Kelso. With wealth came power and titles and John Kerr, first Duke of Roxburghe built Floors Castle at Kelso in the 18th century.

Most other landowners were not of noble rank and were known under the general titles of lairds and *bonnet lairds*. Some held land directly from the crown but most were sub-tenants of the nobility. The Pringles of Torwoodlee (descendants of the more powerful Pringles of Galashiels) acquired land around Galashiels and were among the ranks of the lesser landowners, wealthy merchants and substantial office-holders that made up a rising middle class.

The majority of these held their land under a type of tenure known as "feuferme". This was obtained by paying a large sum of money (grassum) to a feudal superior as a down payment, followed by a rent known as "feu-duty". This type of landholding had originated in the late Middle Ages when the crown and the church both needed to generate income quickly. As land was often feued in large blocks, the cost of purchasing a feuferme charter included a correspondingly large grassum and feu-duties, although the latter were usually set at an economical level initially. However, in such rural areas as the Borders, bonnet lairds, equivalent to Yeoman farmers in England, were able to purchase smaller properties.

These three groups – nobles, lairds and bonnet lairds – were the only members of society who enjoyed "heritable tenure", that is, could pass their property on to their heirs. All three lived primarily off rents, but bonnet lairds had to supplement these by labouring with their own hands. Rents were either paid in cash or in kind, depending on the type of farm and its location, and could represent perhaps as much as one third of a tenant's total output. Apart from this income, the landowner would also provide services or facilities to the tenants for which he would receive additional payments in produce or in labour.

As the 16th century progressed the wealthier landowners sought greater degrees of comfort and Cowdenknowes (Earlston), Huttonhall (now Hutton Castle), Traquair and Ferniehirst (Jedburgh) were built or enlarged from smaller tower houses. This also served to distinguish the older nobility from the newly arrived gentry, who built towers to proclaim the status that came with their newly found wealth. Bonnet lairds built fortified farmsteads (bastles), not only for status, but also for protection from the increasing lawlessness of the border.

After King James VI acceded to the English throne in 1603, to become the first ruler of both Scotland and England, there was a crackdown on the lawless elements which were endemic in the Borders. Consequently, as the Border country became more peaceful during the 17th century, more landowners moved out of their towers and bastles and into new houses that provided comfort and reflected both their status in society and the more peaceful times in which they lived. Nisbet House (Edrom: **fig.9**), Lessudden House (St Boswells), Mertoun Old Hall (now the head gardeners cottage) are examples which still survive, while Pirn House

# Farm and Factory: Revolution in the Borders

***Fig.9** In 1630 Sir Alexander Nisbet of that Ilk demolished Nisbet Castle and built a manor house more appropriate to the greater security which followed the Union of the Crowns in 1603.*

(Innerleithen), Torwoodlee Tower (Galashiels), Redbraes Castle (Polwarth) and many others are now ruined or demolished. The resources to build such houses increased as landowners felt the benefits of investment in agricultural improvement or industry.

Even amongst the peasantry there were social strata defined by relative wealth. Tenants held their farm or shared in a joint tenancy directly from a landowner in a similar arrangement to that through which a nobleman might hold land directly from the king. Husbandmen either held short term leases of between one to six years or were "*tenants-at-will*". Some of these tenant farmers (or husbandmen) were relatively affluent and supported employees of inferior social status to themselves.

Many of these employees would be cottars who typically possessed a cottage and *kailyard*, a small amount of land on the infield and the right to graze a few animals on the outfield or moor.

Cottars did not hold a lease of any kind, were universally tenants-at-will and paid their rent in the form of labour on the husbandman's farm.

Below the social level of cottar were landless labourers and indoor farm servants who worked in return for little more than their board and lodgings, which included meals. None of these men and women had any legal rights to the land upon which they stayed and worked.

At Springwood Park (Kelso) archaeological excavations in 1985-6 revealed the remains of a row of single-storey medieval rectangular *cruck*-built houses with floor drains and open hearths. A row of comparable structures was excavated at Lilliesleaf in 2000, showing that the scale and construction techniques of house building had not altered significantly between the 14$^{th}$ and the 17$^{th}$ century. It is clear that as late as the 17$^{th}$ century people living on a farm were still accommodated under the same thatched roof as their animals. A cottar's home was smaller and less impressive than that of a bonnet laird or husbandman and usually consisted of a single roomed structure containing a few pieces of furniture.

Tenants and cottars were expected to build their own homes with whatever materials were available locally. Stones turned up from the soil by ploughing often served for foundations and these were cemented with clay or laid alternately with turf to form the lower walls. Where clay was plentiful it sometimes formed the main walling material. The upper parts of the walls were often of turf construction. The roof was covered with turf, straw or heather thatch and its weight was carried by pairs of crucks. In a largely treeless countryside timber was in short supply and landowners were often unwilling to provide new roof beams, expecting their tenants to shore up existing rotten timbers with odd pieces of wood.

By the 18th century tenant farmers were more prosperous and housing conditions had improved. Most houses were still thatched structures lit only by a few small windows, often with a midden right outside the front door. Inside they were divided into two main rooms, the "but and ben". The but was a kitchen and servants' apartment where the entire household met at mealtimes. The ben was the farmer's private quarters where he and his family slept at night and entertained friends. A low attic, reached by a ladder rather than a proper stair, provided storage and sleeping accommodation for male farm servants. Open hearth fires tended to be replaced by a fireplace built into one gable with a chimney to carry away the smoke, with the result that the atmosphere indoors was much cleaner. This was not universal and at Lilliesleaf the open hearth had remained in the centre of the floor of one cottage into the later 19th century. The normal labourers' houses in Peeblesshire during the 18th century were sparsely furnished single-room buildings. If the labourer was fortunate enough to afford a cow, the animal shared this single room with the family, occupying a narrow area at one end partitioned off behind the box-beds.

The impact of agricultural change was to dispossess the poorer husbandmen and cottars but to consolidate those farms which remained. By the mid-19th century there were new methods of farming, new types of farm, the beginnings of a farming class and a great reduction in the rural population. The old subsistence farms vanished and were replaced with new, commercially operated farms. It became possible for tenant farmers to acquire long-term leases as landowners sought to consolidate their land. Forward thinking landowners favoured tenant farmers that showed interest and aptitude for the new agricultural methods. With these new leases, larger farms to manage and expanding urban markets for their produce the tenant farmer prospered and his lifestyle changed accordingly.

The new landscape of highly commercialised farming was organised around farmsteads of improved design. In the Lothians and the Merse the mixed arable and livestock farms were the largest lowland farms in Scotland, often running to hundreds of hectares. Their outbuildings and steadings were correspondingly grand. During the 18th century the simple farmhouses and outbuildings of earlier periods were replaced by better built, more spacious and more efficiently laid out farmsteads, which in turn were extended and remodelled during the 19th century.

The improvement of farm workers' accommodation took second place to that for farmers and their animals. However, by the early 19th century squalid cottar houses were beginning to give way to decently built single storey cottages with solid walls of sandstone rubble and *pantiled* roofs. Some farm workers were unmarried and lived a rough existence in communal bothies among the outbuildings. However, it was more common to employ married farm workers and to give them decent housing.

# Farm and Factory: Revolution in the Borders

These new farming methods were not, however, without their price. As landowners consolidated holdings and enclosed the common fields there were fewer opportunities to hold a tenancy. Tenants lost arable holdings to sheep farming when the landlord decided that this was more profitable. As a result, many former tenants became landless, as did cottars. If other employment or tenancy was not available on the land these displaced men and women turned their cottage industry skills to use by moving to rapidly growing towns and new mills.

Rural cottage industries formed the basis of the Industrial Revolution and gradually disappeared as manufacturing became focused on towns. Rural communities still needed local services, however, and some dispossessed husbandmen and cottars were able to find work as rural tradesmen or carriers of supplies from the towns. By 1866 in the village of Lilliesleaf (population 325 in 1861) there were: twenty-five farmers, two cattle dealers, seven grocers, one flesher, one baker, two tailors, three shoemakers, two millwrights, two publicans, one draper, one clothier, one carter, one mole catcher, two joiners, two masons, two blacksmiths and one saddler and ironmonger. Greater direct accessibility to the sources of supply, through public transport and motor cars, has reduced the self-sufficiency of such rural communities. By 2000 (population approx. 225), in addition to the farming community, Lilliesleaf contained two public houses, one post office and shop, one hairdresser and one garage.

## The Urban Population

The 18th century saw much financial speculation. Some made their fortunes in the developing British Empire and when they returned home bought estates appropriate to their new wealth. James Chisholme and Robert Waugh both had successful interests in Jamaica. Chisholme returned and bought Hobsburn House (Hobkirk), which he renamed Greenriver after his plantation in Jamaica and Waugh returned to his native Melrose to build Harmony Hall. Others invested in industry at home and thus contributed to the growth of Borders towns. The Pringle family of Galashiels, for example, helped to fund many of the developments in the town, the population of which grew from 591 in 1755 to 7,500 by the 1860s. Although such investment by local landowners brought them wealth, the greatest fortunes were made by industrialists based in the towns who, in due course, bought estates in the country and themselves became country landowners.

These wealthy industrialists and their backers brought new industries and technologies to the Borders. It was due to their shrewd business sense and desire for progress that small medieval settlements expanded into the towns of today. With wealth came influence and power by which such men moved naturally into important positions in local government and other bodies.

## The urban poor

The population growth which Borders towns and villages experienced in the 18th and 19th centuries was partly due to a better survival rate among the population as a whole, but also due to the movement of people to find work. Traditionally, weaving and other industries had been part-time activities carried out in cottages during quiet periods in the farming calendar. Reorganisation of farmland and farming methods released large numbers of former farm workers without a fall in the quantity of foodstuffs produced, so that fewer people were still able to meet the food demands of an increasing number of consumers. This enabled manufacturers to employ for the first time a large, full-time workforce of all ages.

The developing textile industry in the Borders was able to make use of new inventions, particularly Arkwright's water frame (1768), Hargreaves' *spinning jenny* (1774) and Crompton's mule (1779). Where water power was insufficient to drive machinery, there was now the revolutionary condensing steam engine which James Watt patented in 1769. By employing water or steam power, and not bodily strength to work machinery, manufacturers opened the way for women and even children to work in the factories with the added attraction that they were cheaper to employ.

The "Factory System" employed in the mills operated all year round and the noise and confined atmosphere were in stark contrast to outdoor work. Farm workers were used to long hours, but in the mills conditions made work shifts of twelve to fourteen hours a day for six days of the week far more arduous and initially it was difficult to induce men to work along side women and children. Various ploys were used to attract men, for example by employing them as masons, carpenters, mechanics, handloom weavers working from home, or as overseers on the factory floor.

To accommodate the growing population in the Borders' woollen centres the mill owners built housing for their workers as well as larger houses for themselves. The workers' houses were usually well-built but almost always cramped terraced houses, some of which were provided with gardens or drying greens. Many houses of this type can still be seen in Galashiels and Hawick and to a lesser extent in places such as Innerleithen and Walkerburn (Innerleithen). The facilities that were available in the late 18th and early 19th centuries were, almost without exception, dependent upon private companies, societies or individuals. In the 1780s Alexander Brodie, a native of Innerleithen returned from having made his fortune in England and built a mill and a workhouse at his own expense in the town to provide work for the townspeople.

Although for many industrial housing was an improvement on the rustic hovels that they hailed from, town planning as such was at its most basic and there was neither understanding of, nor adequate provision for public health. Lack of suitable provision for drainage and clean drinking water put town dwellers at a disadvantage to their country cousins. Since the earliest times open drains, street middens and cesspools had made towns ideal breeding grounds for such diseases as bubonic plague, typhoid, typhus, smallpox and diphtheria. As the towns grew these diseases became far more prevalent (**Plate 5**).

The countryside was by no means free from disease, but there was less danger of contamination of drinking water. Even so, malaria or "ague" was a hazard of marshy areas. In the parish of Eccles in the 1790s, for example

*"...the people are peculiarly obnoxious to diseases of debility, such as agues, nervous fevers, chronic rheumatisms, &c. Within these last 20 years, these diseases were almost epidemic... of late, however, they are much less frequent... This may be attributed to... the advanced state of agricultural improvements, and especially of draining the land...".*

This may also have coincided with a general cooling of the Northern Hemisphere from 1780 to around 1815 and it was in this period that malaria appears to have disappeared from Scotland as a whole. By the 18th century, the disease that caused the most problems was smallpox. It was reckoned that under favourable conditions only one in seven children would succumb to it, but if a particularly strong strain appeared the ratio could be one in three. Even before improvements were made to towns the need to deal with this virulent pestilence was recognised and in 1796 an English doctor, Edward Jenner, devised a vaccination. This was rapidly adopted in Scotland and by the 1820s the disease was effectively under control and finally wiped out in Britain during the 20th century and eradicated world-wide in 1979.

The health of the population was also influenced by general improvements in living conditions. Supplies of water, gas and electricity were developed to meet the needs of the growing population. Private water companies were founded in Galashiels in 1839, Jedburgh and

# Farm and Factory: Revolution in the Borders

Peebles in 1845 and these were amongst the first communities to benefit. Others had to wait; at Kelso and Hawick in 1866 the water supply and sewerage systems were still under construction. At Hawick the cost was anticipated to be £9,000 and would have been raised by public subscription. Prior to this wells provided water for the settlements and whilst these would be fairly safe in the countryside, town supplies could easily be contaminated. Provision of clean water was fundamental for the elimination of diseases such as cholera which struck Hawick and Kelso in 1832 and Hawick again in 1849. Such enterprises were funded by private individuals, often at considerable cost to themselves.

Lighting in factories and better-off households was improved even before clean water or sewerage were supplied. Large country houses such as Bowhill and Marchmont had their own gas works as early as the 1820s, although in some cases such as at Abbotsford (Melrose) these were short lived. In towns private companies were set up to supply coal gas by subscription, initially to factories and the wealthier town houses. Two of the earliest urban companies to be funded were in Duns (1825) and Peebles (1829) and many others followed in the 1830s and 1840s. In time, the gas network was extended to supply street lighting and reach less wealthy homes.

The rate at which these changes occurred was influenced by a series of Victorian Police Acts, under which a widening range of communities could carry out schemes to address law and order, street lighting, pavements, sewerage and water supply. Communities acted at varying pace under these Acts. By 1866 the village of Chirnside (population: 1,502) had it's own gas company, whereas in the town of Galashiels (population: 3,379), where dry summers invariably produced drought and some wells were infected by cesspools, many people still lacked access to clean water.

Although industry provided work, real social progress in the 19th century was slow and came about in part as a gradual reflection of the increased national prosperity. Parish responsibility for the poor was reflected in Borders towns by the establishment of charitable societies such as the Ladies Clothing Societies and Industrial Ragged Schools. Combination or Union Poorhouses (**fig.10**) were set up to

*Fig.10*  The Combination Poorhouse at Hawick, opened in 1857, provided work for the poorest members of society. Until recently it housed Drumlanrig Hospital.

## Farm and Factory: Revolution in the Borders

| Name | Town of Birth | Area of Expertise |
|---|---|---|
| Ainslie, John (1745-1828) | Jedburgh | Cartographer |
| Bogue, David (1750-1825) | Coldingham | Co-founder of the London Missionary Society and founder of the British and Foreign Bible Society |
| Brewster, Sir David (1781-1868) | Jedburgh | Inventor of the Kaleidoscope, Stereoscope and Lithoscope |
| Broadwood, John (1732-1812) | Cockburnspath | Founder of the London pianoforte house Tschudi and Broadwood |
| Brunlees, Sir James (1816-92) | Kelso | Civil Engineer |
| Brunton, Sir Thomas Lauder (1844-1916) | Roxburgh | Pharmacologist |
| Chambers, William (1800-83) | Peebles | Publisher |
| Fairbairn, Sir William (1789-1874) | Kelso | Engineer and Inventor |
| Fortune, Robert (1813-80) | Edrom | Horticulturist |
| Herbertson, Andrew John (1865-1915) | Galashiels | Geographer |
| Lee, James Paris (1831-1904) | Hawick | Inventor of the Lee-Enfield Rifle |
| Mackenzie, Charles Frederick (1825-62) | Portmore, Peebles | First Bishop of Central Africa and Equality Proponent |
| Morrison, Robert (1782-1834) | Jedburgh | Scholar and Missionary |
| Mungo Park (1771-1806) | Foulshiels, Selkirk | Explorer of Africa |
| Murray, Sir James Augustus Henry (1837-1915) | Denholm | Lexicographer and Editor of what was to become the Oxford English Dictionary |
| Nichol, James (1810-79) | Traquair | Geologist |
| Pringle, Sir John (1707-82) | Stitchill | Father of Modern Military Medicine. His idea lead to the establishment of the Red Cross |
| Rutherford, Prof. William (1839-99) | Ancrum Craig | Physiologist |
| Small, James (c.1740-93) | Upsettlington | Inventor |
| Somerville, Mary (1780-1872) | Jedburgh | Mathematician and Scientist |
| Wilson, James (1805-60) | Hawick | Founder of the *Economist* |

*Fig.11* Famous Borderers.

serve towns and surrounding communities; that at Peebles now houses a Scottish Borders Council area office. Sickness benefit and funeral expenses could be insured for through Sick and Burial Societies, which existed in every town. In 1866 Kelso had five different sick and burial insurance clubs, while Hawick had seven. Abstinence Societies also existed in every town to combat alcoholism and thereby reduce social misery in the interests of domestic and public order and general health.

Education was more widely available in Scotland than in England, which placed Scots at an advantage in filling posts in the developing British Empire. Through proximity to England, Borderers had more immediate access to news and information from the south. It is not surprising, therefore, that the region counts a number of pioneers, thinkers and inventors among its former residents (**fig.11**).

With a growing level of literacy, demand for reading matter grew. The Kelso Chronicle was printed from 1832 and subscription libraries were set up in towns and villages as a source of wider learning. The period saw the growth of special interest societies, such as the Border Society, now the Border Union Agricultural Society (1812); the Berwickshire Naturalist's Club (1831) and Hawick Archaeological Society (1856); all three are still active. A whole range of such groups covered topics ranging from the arts (including town bands, choral and literary societies), horticulture and livestock (such as the "Border Counties Society for Improvement of Domestic Poultry, Pigeons and Canaries" of Jedburgh) to angling and other sports. A ploughing match was held at Jedburgh in 1786 and this led the way for the foundation of Ploughing Societies in many Borders farming communities and encouraged that particular skill among arable workers. Lodges of Freemasons were not new and St John's Lodge in Melrose claimed to have been founded by John Morow, the medieval architect who worked on parts of Melrose Abbey. A lodge of the Independent Order of Oddfellows was founded at Kelso in 1841.

Outdoor recreation was, and still is, an important aspect of Borders life, although long working hours for the working classes created a bias towards middle-class interests. Curling was a traditional pastime and Hawick Curling Society dated from 1740, but the very nature of the sport required cold winters to sustain it and many curling ponds became overgrown and abandoned in the 20$^{th}$ century. Kelso was a resort for Edinburgh gentry and its racecourse, still in operation, was established in 1822. The mid-19$^{th}$ century saw the establishment of many urban sporting societies of the more leisurely variety, such as angling, bowls, cricket, and quoits. Hawick was the first Borders town to have its own rugby team (1873) and others soon followed at Galashiels (1875), Melrose (1877) with teams at Earlston, Walkerburn and Kelso by 1886. Soccer teams were also established, although they lacked the enthusiastic support that Borderers reserved for rugby, and by the end of the 19$^{th}$ century golf was also becoming popular.

Improvements in communications, in particular the arrival of the railways, gave access to cheaper food and coal. The 19$^{th}$ century also saw a gradual improvement in pay and working conditions, partly through the influence of trade unions. These were not always permanent societies. In 1889 the dyers of Hawick formed a union to fight for a pay rise; once this rise had been secured the union was dissolved. Workers could bring pressure to bear on their employers. In 1900 at the mills of P & R Sanderson (Galashiels) workers unhappy at staffing levels won their demands by refusing to urinate in the receptacles provided, thus depriving the scouring department of its principal supply of ammonia.

By the end of the 19$^{th}$ century the towns were very different places from those which had existed a century before. There were running water, gas and electricity, police and fire services, public schools and hospitals, all of which had arisen through the need to provide for the growing urban population. Throughout the 20th century the technology of the textile mills grew more sophisticated. Unfortunately this did not always benefit the workers, who found themselves replaced by machines. Other factors have also influenced this sector of the Borders economy, most important being the increasing globalisation of trade. This has led to a severe decline in the textile industry in the Borders and those mills still in operation focus on the more exclusive segment of the market for their goods.

## Food and drink

The main impact of the Agricultural Revolution was a massive increase in the quantity and quality of foodstuffs which it made possible. These not only created greater variety of eating, they supported the growth of a larger and mainly town-based population.

Historically the aristocracy spurned vegetables in favour of meat, whereas the peasantry could afford to eat meat only occasionally. Agricultural improvements, technological developments in food processing and the growth of the British Empire brought a wider range of foodstuffs to ordinary families.

### *Meat and dairy produce*

Even in towns it was common for people to keep livestock. Pigs were particularly popular since they could be fattened on household waste and no part of the carcass would be wasted. Uncured joints, sausages and puddings which would perish if not eaten at once were shared with neighbours and the rest - hams, gammons and bacon - would be salted for longer term consumption. In winter beasts were traditionally slaughtered and consumed when there was not enough fodder to feed them. During the 18th century the need for this practice diminished as the increased growth in production of cereals and root vegetables such as turnip provided fodder during the winter months.

The nobility had access to a wider range of domesticated and game animals. Venison and hare also provided recreational opportunities for the chase.

New varieties of stock were also introduced and the traditional types were, in many cases, improved. The results were much larger animals than older domesticated varieties and yielded much more meat. These experiments were spread throughout the Borders from the Berwickshire coast to the upper reaches of the Tweed. The minister of Cockburnspath was able to report in 1793 that "*the full Northumberland breed [of sheep] has been lately tried with great success...*". Similarly the ministers of Eckford and Oxnam in Teviotdale respectively noted that "*black cattle are generally of a good size, being bred from large English bulls*" and "*...the sheep have been greatly improved of late...by purchasing tups from Northumberland and other counties in England...*".

Rabbits were a cheap source of meat and King Malcolm IV granted the earliest recorded royal charter for a man-made warren in Scotland to Coldingham Priory in the 1150s. Warrens developed as an additional food source up to the 18th century, by the end of which escapees had reproduced to become an agricultural nuisance, although they continued to provide an important additional meat source up to the introduction of myxamotosis in the 1950s.

Meat should be eaten quickly, particularly in warm weather, and salting or smoking to preserve it has an effect on the flavour. The medieval spice trade flourished because spices hid the bad flavour of rotting meat. The problems of extending the life of foodstuffs was tackled in the 18th century by ice houses built by the wealthy to store winter snow and examples still survive at Kimmerghame (Edrom), Black Barony (Eddleston) and Marchmont. The basic problems were solved by the French, who invented food canning (1810) and the refrigerator (1859). Although it took many years before canned foods were in common use throughout society (the tin-opener was not invented until 1859), meat ceased to be the virtual monopoly of the wealthy, particularly once frozen lamb started to arrive from Australia and New Zealand on refrigerated ships after 1880. Cured meats continued to appeal, but the process became centralised and much was carried out at Kelso, where more than 4,000 carcasses were cured in 1865-66.

## *Poultry*

A wide variety of wild birds and their eggs have been eaten since ancient times, particularly water fowl and sea birds, such as bitterns and heron inland and gannets and kittiwakes on the coast. Only varieties of duck continue to feature commonly on menus today, and the swans of Berwick upon Tweed are no longer eaten. Other game birds such as pheasant and partridge are still managed especially for shooting. The staple poultry of the farmyard were chickens, geese, turkeys and pigeons.

Pigeons were the most plentiful as they were content to live in large flocks in doocots (dovecotes), where they provided landowners with a source of food all year round. The birds' droppings provided a useful by-product as fertiliser. Pigeons were eaten in a variety of ways including being baked in pots with claret and sealed with butter (the latter could keep for as long as three months). Although they had a natural tendency to roost together and the doocot provided a convenient home, the birds were not confined to the farmyard and ranged widely in search of food in newly sown fields and gardens. This brought complaints from neighbours and on occasion this resentment would erupt into acts of revenge, including killing of the birds and destruction of the doocots. A series of increasingly severe laws were passed to combat this, and by the end of the 16th century repeat offenders faced no less than the death penalty.

Although the pigeons themselves benefited from the agricultural improvements and allegedly ate enough grain to feed 3,000 people in Midlothian in 1796, more effective husbandry reduced the dependence on pigeons for winter meat. Hens provided bigger eggs and farmyard dung was more plentiful and just as effective. Although doocots continued to be used well into the 19th century their importance waned and some were even converted for other uses. For instance, a doocot at Stow became a bothy for navvies building the Edinburgh to Galashiels road and another at Mellerstain was turned into a cottage orneé (**Plate 6**).

## *Fish*

There were fishponds at Dryburgh Abbey and Eccles Priory in medieval times and most communities engaged in fishing whether inland or on the Berwickshire coast. Although nets caught more fish, the skill required for rod fishing, and the quality of Tweed salmon in particular, made the area attractive to sportsmen and was the origin in the mid-19th century of community angling societies. A fishing *shiel* typical of those used by anglers on the lower Tweed is still visible at Paxton.

In the 12th century Eyemouth was founded as a fishing community to serve Coldingham Priory. However, it was not until after the enclosure of the common fields in 1763 that the town really began to develop. The construction of stone piers between 1747 and 1769 improved the harbour and was followed by an increase in trade, especially corn, and the establishment in the town of merchants dealing in foreign goods.

The fishing industry of the town developed rapidly in the 19th century with the chief focus of the industry being the provision of herring to the immediate hinterland, although any surplus was either sent to London or even abroad. Improvements to the harbour provided an impetus for dramatic developments in the fishing industry. So much so, that the minister of the parish was able to record that between 1809 and 1820, no less than 10,000 barrels of herring were brought into the port yearly.

The importance of salt water fishing to other parts of the Borders is illustrated by the "*Herring Road*", an old path over the Lammermuir Hills to Lauder by which route the inhabitants of Lauderdale were able to bring barrels of smoked herring from the coast.

## Cereals and Vegetables

Bread still forms the traditional basic diet of Borderers in spite of the alternatives which are now available. In the 18th century the rich ate bread made from wheat while the peasantry ate a poor sort of bread made from *bere*, a primitive form of barley. This distinction gradually disappeared as more effective production brought down the price of wheat.

In 1698 Patrick and Grisell Home, Earl and Countess of Marchmont hosted a table that included potage, beef, lobster, pigeon, chicken, mutton, rabbits, kid, "wild fowl", geese, lamb, skate, jelly, tarts and green salad, with claret, sherry, gin and port. Bread is not mentioned, but would also have been available.

By contrast, the average household of the Earl's tenants is likely to have dined on bread, vegetables and a little meat, such as bacon or rabbit, washed down with beer. The beer was a necessity, not a luxury, due to the doubtful quality of drinking water. Each farm or community brewed it's own ale and sometimes rented the facilities necessary from a nearby owner. Prior to 1560 Kelso Abbey had numerous breweries on its estates from which the monks received rent and the peasants brewed ale from the bere that they grew.

With the improvements a wide range of new foodstuffs was cultivated, although few were grown directly for the benefit of the poorer members of society. New experimental crops included turnips, carrots and potatoes, all common today, but exotic novelties in the 18th century. These new crops were soon adopted, particularly the potato, which was to become a staple part of the diet.

## *Fruit*

In addition to new varieties of vegetables, experiments were also carried out with fruits. The tradition of the controlled cultivation of fruit was not new for there were walled gardens in Scotland in the early 16th century. By the late 17th century Sir Robert Sibbald catalogued over 400 species of plants and fruits that were grown in Scotland in his work "*Scotia Illustrata*". The walled gardens of the 18th and 19th centuries, however, did much to compensate for any shortcomings in the climate. South-facing walls received more sun and were the ideal place to grow *espalier* fruit trees. Varieties of plants from warmer climates could be grown in glasshouses and the garden walls were constructed with internal flues so that warm temperatures could be maintained by a fire even when the weather turned cool. A curious example is Tweed Vineries which was established at Clovenfords (Caddonfoot) in 1869, substantially added to the size of the settlement and closed in 1959.

The region has traditionally grown a variety of fruits, including apples, pears and plums. In 1798 Kelso, Melrose, Gattonside (Melrose) and Jedburgh were well known for their orchards. Jedburgh, in particular, was famous for its pears and some examples are still grown in Greyfriars Garden in the town (**Plate 7**) and a wide variety of apples is still grown in the Priorwood Gardens (Melrose). Walled gardens and imperial exploration enabled land owners to grow an increasing variety of produce. To native soft fruits such as strawberries, currants and gooseberries were added, in time, rhubarb, apricots, peaches, melons, citrus fruits and figs. Walled gardens can still be seen at Kailzie (Traquair), Linthill (Lilliesleaf), Floors Castle (Kelso), Manderston (Edrom) and Wilton Park (Hawick). Such gardens also grew herbs, now used more for flavouring dishes rather than for their medicinal properties.

## Communications

Agriculture and industry were only able to progress because their development went hand in hand with improvements in transport. This had a huge impact on the ability of people and goods to move around the country and beyond its frontiers. New transport networks were created and in some cases superseded by further innovations. Many old roads, most of the railway network and a number of small harbours have been abandoned but are still prominent in the landscape. In other cases, lines of movements have remained in everyday use although the transport systems using them have been upgraded. Thus many modern roads follow the course of 18th century turnpikes, while the main railway line from Berwick to Edinburgh and Glasgow still uses the route laid out by the first generation of railway engineers. The desire for improved communications was so great that, in 1792, proposals were developed to build a canal from Berwick to Ancrum. Although this scheme was never implemented it illustrates all methods were considered when attempts were being made to improve the communications network in the Borders.

## *Old Roads*

Most of the roads that are visible in the landscape relate to recent periods of heavy use. Before the 18th century road transport was, as throughout the rest of Scotland, slow, difficult and expensive. Because of physical difficulties and because the country was comparatively poor, few wheeled vehicles were in use before the 18th century except in the immediate vicinity of the larger towns. Pack horses carried most goods, including bulky items like grain and coal. Over short distances sleds were often preferred to carts. Their lower centre of gravity made them safer on steep slopes. They were used for bringing peat down from the hills, stone from the quarries, or sheaves of grain from the fields to the stack-yard.

Outside the towns most roads were merely bands of intertwining trackways worn by repeated use. They narrowed at river crossings and between obstructions, such as the policy walls around country houses, and fanned out through open country as each traveller chose his own path.

In heavily cultivated lowlands there are few traces of old roads as they have either been incorporated into modern ones or have been obliterated by cultivation. In more marginal hill areas, however, many old roads can still be traced. A particularly good example survives at Outer Cock Law (Morebattle). In such areas traffic tended to follow the hills rather than the valleys. The ridges were better drained and movement along them was easier than the settled valley floors. In such terrain old roads often appear as terraces where they cross hillsides and as deeply cut hollow ways where they climb steeper slopes.

A number of old roads cross the Lammermuir Hills. One of the best known is the *"Herring Road"* between Lothian Edge near Spott and the head of the Dye Water towards the Leader. As the name suggests, the inhabitants of the central Tweed valley used it in the 17th and 18th centuries to carry pack horse loads of salt herring from Dunbar for the winter. The so-called *"Thieves' Road"* in the Tweedsmuir Hills was improved in places by careful construction. These sections were clearly upgraded for wheeled vehicles before the establishment of a full network of turnpikes opened up the surrounding valleys for carts and wagons and caused the ridgeway routes to fall out of use.

The "drove road" was a specialised kind of road which saw use in the 17th, 18th and 19th centuries, when large numbers of Scottish cattle and sheep were driven to England to meet the ever-rising demand for fresh meat. Originally many of these animals came from the Borders themselves, but by the later 17th century increasing numbers

## *Farm and Factory: Revolution in the Borders*

were being reared in the Highlands. They were driven through the Borders to the industrial north of England, while others were sent further south for the London market. By the end of the 17th century over 30,000 cattle a year were crossing the Border and in the 18th century the numbers rose far higher. The coming of the railways allowed livestock to be transported far more quickly and easily than on the hoof and this brought about a rapid decline in the droving trade, which was all but a memory by the close of the 19th century.

One of the most important drove routes crossed the Pentland Hills to Romannobridge (Newlands), after which different routes led to the English Border. The drove road from Peebles over Kirkhope Law (Peebles/ Traquair) still runs between stone *dykes* designed to contain the animals on the hoof. The cattle were rested each night at regular 'stances' and there were inns to cater for the passing trade; a number of modern Border inns and hotels originated in this way.

### *Road Bridges*

There are more than 1200 bridges in use over Borders rivers today and these include many that were built before the 19th century. When the Tweed Bridge at Peebles was built in the 15th century the only other bridge downstream was at Old Roxburgh, the earlier medieval bridge between Birgham and Carham having decayed. In the 16th century an unusual bridge was built near Lowood (Melrose), possibly by the Pringle family. This also decayed in time, and its remains were described in 1743 in these terms:

*"It has been a Timber Bridge; in the middle Pillar there has been a Chain for a Drawbridge, with a little House for the Conveniency of those that kept the Bridge and received the Custom."*

This toll bridge may have gone out of use because people were not prepared to pay the tolls, using instead the Salter's Ford some way downstream. All the Borders rivers *can* be forded, but a dry crossing is far more convenient and reliable, particularly in periods of spate.

***Fig.12*** *Canongate Bridge in Jedburgh was the principal entry on the south side of the town and carried the road from England. The oldest surviving structure was a narrow packhorse bridge without parapets, but in the 16th century stone from the Franciscan friary was used to extend this into a wider bridge with parapets.*

# Farm and Factory: Revolution in the Borders

Prior to the construction of Berwick Bridge in 1611-34 the lower reaches of the Tweed could have only been crossed by boat. There was no bridge at Kelso from the destruction of the medieval bridge at Roxburgh in the 16th century until 1754. A lack of investment before the 17th and 18th centuries must have caused much inconvenience and been an obstacle to movement about the countryside.

Many bridges were financed by burghs in their own interest as a way of improving access to their markets and fairs. Peebles Burgh Council paid for a stone bridge over the Eddleston Water in 1465, probably to replace an earlier wooden one. At Jedburgh the Canongate Bridge (**fig.12**) over the Jedwater was widened in the 16th century using stone quarried from monastic houses in the town. There was no central control, however, over bridge building and the first approach to a strategic network came with the establishment of Turnpike Trusts in the 18th century.

In Roxburghshire and Selkirkshire alone twenty-four major new bridges were constructed between 1764 and 1813. As the techniques of bridge building advanced, engineers developed flatter, broader spans and used hollow arches and piers to produce lighter, more delicate structures without sacrificing strength. Two of the grandest examples are James Smeaton's bridge across the Tweed at Coldstream, opened in 1767 and John Rennie's Kelso Bridge, opened in 1803. Kelso Bridge was the model for Rennie's later Waterloo Bridge in London and has pairs of *Doric* columns above the *cutwaters*.

Smaller bridges followed the trends set by the great designers, though for many purposes plain single-span rubble bridges were perfectly adequate. Where the stone was suitable, quite large spans were rubble-built. In its day Ashiestiel Bridge (Caddonfoot) at 40m (131ft) was the longest single span rubble-arched bridge in the world.

New materials were used in bridge construction

*Fig.13* Union Suspension Bridge was designed by Capt. Sir Samuel Brown and opened in 1820. It is Europe's oldest surviving suspension bridge carrying road traffic.

from around 1810. Cast iron was used throughout the 19th century for small and medium sized bridges. In the major spans of the later 19th century, cast-iron was used for the outer girders only, the main weight of the carriageway and traffic being carried on wrought iron or steel girders of arch form. Capt. Sir Samuel Brown of the Royal Navy, was the pioneer of the use of iron in suspension chains or cables. His greatest work is probably the Union Bridge (Hutton), which like several smaller bridges, such as those at Kalemouth (Eckford) and Gattonside footbridge at Melrose, has a wooden deck and chain links forged from iron bars (**fig.13**). This is the oldest suspension bridge in Europe that still carries cars. Brown's method of iron construction was used widely in mid-19th century bridges, but other types also existed, for instance the lenticular (lens-shaped) truss type found in a footbridge at Roxburgh

Viaduct. The most important later 19th and 20th century construction was the lattice- or plate-girder bridge, which was relatively rare in iron but fairly common in steel, for instance at Walkerburn.

Concrete bridges in Britain date in the main from the 1920s, and in the interwar period took a profusion of forms. In the early 1930s design had stabilised to some extent, and concrete 'arch' bridges were more or less standard. Sometimes designers covered the 'bones' of such bridges in masonry. More recent major road bridges of concrete construction were opened across the Tweed at Galashiels in 1975, Leaderfoot in 1973 and Kelso in 1998.

## *Turnpikes*

The bridges at Coldstream, Kelso and Mertoun (by James Slight, 1839-41) all have adjoining tollhouses where travellers made a contribution towards the cost of the bridge and its upkeep in return for its use. Such tolls or "pontage" were also collected at Drygrange Bridge (Melrose). A feature of the 18th century was the application of this same principle to major roads, for which Turnpike Trusts were authorised by Parliament to upgrade roads and recover the cost by levied charges.

The first road to be turnpiked was the Great North Road from Edinburgh to Berwick, testifying to importance of this route. The stretch between Cockburnspath and the border at Lamberton (**Plate 8**) originally followed the historic route over Coldingham Moor and Lamberton Moor until 1790-1810, when the line was altered to pass through Grantshouse (Coldingham) and Burnmouth, most of which is still followed by the modern A1 trunk road.

Turnpikes were so successful that in most cases they form the basis of the modern road network and their former existence can sometimes be detected from surviving turnpike cottages. Examples can be seen on the A698 at Spittal-on-Rule (Cavers), on the B711 at Greenbank Toll (Roberton) and on the A72 at Thornylee (Walkerburn). That more do not survive is due to the stipulations of the original Acts of Parliament, which generally stated that tollhouses should be demolished once the cost of the road had been recovered.

Although successful, turnpikes were resented by local people who found that, not only was their freedom of movement limited by enclosure of the open fields, they were now also expected to pay to use roads where they had previously gone for nothing. In consequence, public anger and outcry often resulted. In one instance a tollhouse planned for the Lauder to Kelso road was abandoned before construction had even begun for fear of public unrest. In 1791-2 opposition to the erection of seven toll bars in and around Duns, particularly two located within the town, was so great that four of them were burnt to the ground. In 1854 Kelso Bridge was the scene of serious rioting when it was alleged that the townsfolk were being forced to pay tolls even after the price of the construction of the bridge had been met. In the ensuing chaos the tollhouse was almost destroyed. In this occasion, however, the rioters appear to have been vindicated as, in the aftermath, a successful prosecution was undertaken against the bridge trustees over the exploitation of the townsfolk. Even so, tolls were still being levied on many Borders roads and on the bridges of Drygrange, Mertoun, Kelso (apparently), Coldstream and Ladykirk in 1866.

Some tolls were particularly lucrative and competition to run them was fierce, however, on quieter roads the toll keeper was obliged to supplement his income in other ways, for example by the sale of alcohol. Although this was illegal without the appropriate licence, the practice was widespread and was often carried out under the noses of the local authorities, despite complaints from the local clergy and innkeepers. Another way, to supplement income was to accommodate couples who could not obtain permission to marry in England.

# Farm and Factory: Revolution in the Borders

Although Gretna Green (Dumfriesshire) is the best known venue for such romantic elopements, marriages were also performed at Lamberton Toll and Coldstream Bridge.

## *Railways*

Although travellers on the improved turnpikes were able to travel more easily and faster over long distances than at any previous time, by the early 19th century speed of travel was still governed by the strength and endurance of horses. The steam-driven railway changed this.

Wagon ways, in which horses pulled trucks along rails, were developed for the coal mining industry in north-east England. In 1810 Thomas Telford was asked to design a cast-iron railway to link Glasgow and Berwick and improve east-west communications. This would not have improved the speed of communications significantly, as there were no locomotives yet developed to pull the wagon and the plans came to nothing.

The first commercial railway was opened at Middleton Colliery, Yorkshire in 1812 and early successors continued to be based on coalfields. Even the Edinburgh to Glasgow line (opened 1842) was originally thought of in this way. From 1825 trains carried passengers and further extended the ability of people to move about. Plans were soon made for a cross border link between southern Scotland and the burgeoning network in northern England. Many schemes for this link were put forward during the early 1840s. In 1844 parliamentary approval was granted for the first trans-border line from Edinburgh to Berwick via the east coast under the Edinburgh and Berwick Railway. It was the plan of the founder, John Learmonth, to annex a huge triangle of country between Edinburgh, Berwick and Carlisle but, like many early railway promoters, he was over-optimistic about the traffic that would be generated in this largely agricultural area with few towns or mineral resources. After this company failed, it was restarted as the North British Railway in 1845 and in 1846 plans for connecting with the Great Northern Railway were made, which led to the building of the Border Railway Bridge over the Tweed.

Construction of the main line from Edinburgh to Dunbar provided few engineering problems but beyond Dunbar the character of the line changed with some difficult streams to cross, like the Dunglass Burn (Cockburnspath), and a steep climb over the fringes of the Lammermuirs to Grantshouse. Trouble also arose about wayleaves and there were problems with the road authorities on rerouting small sections of the road and constructing road and rail bridges.

In addition to the difficulties posed by the terrain there were also labour troubles, including a small riot between Irish navvies from Grantshouse and Highland navvies from Cockburnspath. The riot is thought to have been caused by bad whiskey and poor living conditions, but whatever the cause the people of Cockburnspath locked their doors and sent a message to Dunbar for military help. The local police left the contractors to calm things down themselves, and their report to the Directors describes a scene like a mutinous ship. To add to this trouble, a flood removed the embankment and culvert crossing the Tower Dean, a problem which was to be repeated a century later.

The railway was opened in June 1846 and stagecoach services between Edinburgh and Berwick were immediately abandoned. Heavy rain the following autumn damaged the line and it took serious amounts of money to re-open it. Despite this, some of the original bridges on the line are still in use, notably the six span viaduct at Dunglass and the bridge at Ayton.

Competition between railway companies to establish a route across the Border had intensified in 1841 when there had been a government decision that only one trans-Border line was viable. This proved to be an underestimation of the traffic potential of long-distance lines and by 1850 three Anglo-Scottish routes had been established: the North British Railway East Coast line; the Caledonian's line from Carlisle to Glasgow via Beattock and the Glasgow & South Western line from Glasgow to Carlisle (**fig.24**).

The North British Railway Company was keen to extend its influence to Carlisle and after lobbying parliament, received permission in 1845 to construct a line from Edinburgh to Hawick via Galashiels. This line was opened four years later and the consequent greater availability of cheap coal transformed the technology of the Border textile industries, allowing them to convert to steam power and expand their output. The railways also brought many new workers, notably Irish immigrants, into the Borders. The success of this line meant that branches were built to Kelso, Jedburgh and Selkirk in the 1850s and later to Peebles. By 1855 Peebles was linked directly to Edinburgh by a line *via* Eddleston and as a result of better access the town developed as a fashionable spa resort.

The ultimate goal of the North British Railway was a link from Edinburgh to Carlisle. This was not achieved until 1862 due to opposition from the Caledonian Railway and lack of interest by the Duke of Buccleuch, who owned much of the land south of Hawick. When the line was finally opened it became known as the Waverley Route. The line was expensive to build with numerous embankments and cuttings, several viaducts and the Whitrope Tunnel (Castleton) on the watershed between Teviotdale and Liddesdale. It was on this route that one of the most isolated railway communities in the country, Riccarton Junction (Castleton) was developed, with rows of cottages, a school and a community centre. Riccarton was the point at which the Waverley Route was joined by the Border Counties Railway from North Tyneside and Northumberland.

Once the two main lines had been built via the East Coast and Hawick, a network of branch lines was established in the Borders to connect them. The Berwickshire Railway, completed in 1865, started from the North British terminus at Duns and ran to join the main Hawick to Edinburgh line at Newstead (Melrose). Other branch lines included a short stretch from Burnmouth to Eyemouth and a link between Berwick and Kelso, which provided a second east-west link up the Tweed valley. The Caledonian Railway also had a branch line built through the Biggar Gap to Peebles.

In 1896 an Act was passed encouraging the construction of light railways to serve remote and scattered communities. Because they were not expected to carry heavy traffic they were designed to be built and operated more cheaply than standard railways. The Borders was already well served by conventional branch lines and only one light railway was built. This line, opened in 1901, left the main line to Hawick at Fountainhall (Heriot) in the valley of the Gala Water and crossed the moors to the Leader Water. It was designed to serve the burgh of Lauder.

From c.1900 motor cars and buses provided alternative forms of transport and by the 1930s competition from motor bus services was undermining the viability of some branch lines and the closure of the less profitable ones was inevitable. The lines to Dolphinton and Lauder were closed in the early 1930s. A flood in 1948 damaged embankments and bridges on the Berwickshire railway so badly that the line was never re-opened. Further closures followed in the 1950s with the axing of the lines to Duns and Selkirk. Then came the Beeching era of closures in the 1960s culminating in the axing of the Waverley Route, despite much local opposition, in 1969.

Although the East Coast Main Line still passes through the area (and is the only working railway which does), there are no stations on the stretch which passes through the Borders. The sites of many disused stations are still clear and, at some of them, the station buildings are still in use as

# Farm and Factory: Revolution in the Borders

*Fig.14  Melrose Station was opened in 1849 and is the only substantially preserved railway station in the Borders.*

private homes. The former station at Melrose, the only surviving one on the Waverley Route was refurbished and may still be visited (**fig.14**).

## Harbours

The Berwickshire coast is not well provided with natural harbours and this made the estuary of the Tweed and the port of Berwick hugely important for the distribution of goods from the Borders during the medieval period. Sea trade was equally important for the importation of goods that were not available locally. This was especially the case in the period from the 13th to 16th centuries when trade with England was curtailed due to extended hostilities and warfare. At this time the only other harbours or landing sites that are on record were at Burnmouth and Eyemouth which were both small scale and used mainly by fishermen. With the loss of Berwick in 1482 to the English, other sites which had probably been utilised occasionally in the previous centuries now took on greater importance. Sites which today appear inhospitable and unsuitable as landing sites were used. Gutcher's Hole (Cockburnspath) which is situated immediately to the south-east of the Dunglass Burn is one such site.

Before the 19th century this did not matter greatly because cargo and fishing vessels were small and could operate from havens which were little better than open beaches. The increase in size of ships in the 19th century and competition from railways led to the concentration of trade into fewer large ports. This, and the decline of coastal fisheries, caused many small harbours to be virtually abandoned.

The growth in sea trade in the Borders can only be traced to 1747 when development of the harbour of Eyemouth began with the laying out of the Old Pier. As a result of this and additional work in 1770 Eyemouth became home to many merchants who were described as "*numerous and respectable*". Besides the corn trade which was the primary purpose for the development of the harbour, these merchants opened up trade with the Baltic sea region for products such as timber, iron and pitch. This meant that goods were as readily available here as in Berwick.

Large quantities of corn and meal were shipped up the coast to Leith and other markets. Some of the merchants, like farmers further inland, took a lead in developing improved agricultural methods, such as planting hedges, growing turnips and sowing grass for pasture. The other industry developed as a result of the improved harbour was the herring fishery which reached the peak of its prosperity In the early 19$^{th}$ century. New harbours were built to accommodate fishing vessels in places which had been used by shipping for centuries but which had no proper facilities. Cove Harbour (1831) is a good example and retains much of its 19$^{th}$ century character. The harbour at St Abbs was constructed in 1833, but here the piers have been enclosed by later outer breakwaters to form a more sheltered refuge which is still used by crab and lobster fishermen.

In 1866 fishing on the Berwickshire coast was carried out with full decked boats of about 13-15m (48-55ft) in length for white fish (mainly haddock) and smaller, half decked boats for herring. On the whole coast from Cove to Burnmouth fifty-nine of the former and 185 of the smaller were employed. In the hurricane of 14 October 1881 a total of 189 fishermen were killed, of which 129 were from Eyemouth, twenty-four from Burnmouth, eleven from Cove and three from St Abbs (**fig.15**). The first lifeboat at Eyemouth was the "James and Rachel Grindley", which was berthed there from 1876, but the first motorised lifeboat did not appear until 1937. Other safety measures on the coast included the establishment of the HM Coastguard at Eyemouth in the 1820s and the construction of St Abbs Head lighthouse in 1862.

During the 18$^{th}$ and early 19$^{th}$ centuries smuggling was rife, particularly along the Berwickshire coast, which led to the use of many coves as landing sites. Redheugh (Cockburnspath) 3km (2 miles) west of Fast

***Fig.15*** *The Fishing Disaster Memorial at Eyemouth commemorates the day in 1881 when 189 fishermen drowned in a freak storm.*

Castle (Coldingham), was a notorious smugglers' haunt, so much so that a coastguard station was established in the 1820s, on the cliffs above. The ruins of the coastguards' boathouse by the harbour still remain. Smuggling was not, however, conducted only from remote spots along the coast; there was thriving trade in illicit goods centred around Eyemouth. Whisky was exported to England and imports included tobacco and gin from Holland and wine and brandy from France (**Plate 9**).

Harbours continued to be developed for more conventional purposes through the 19$^{th}$ and into the 20$^{th}$ century. The harbours at Burnmouth and Eyemouth were both improved in the late 19$^{th}$ and mid 20$^{th}$ centuries respectively. Eyemouth, in particular, has undergone many changes and improvements in the interest of the herring fishery with notable redevelopment occurring in 1965 and 1996-98.

# Part 3:

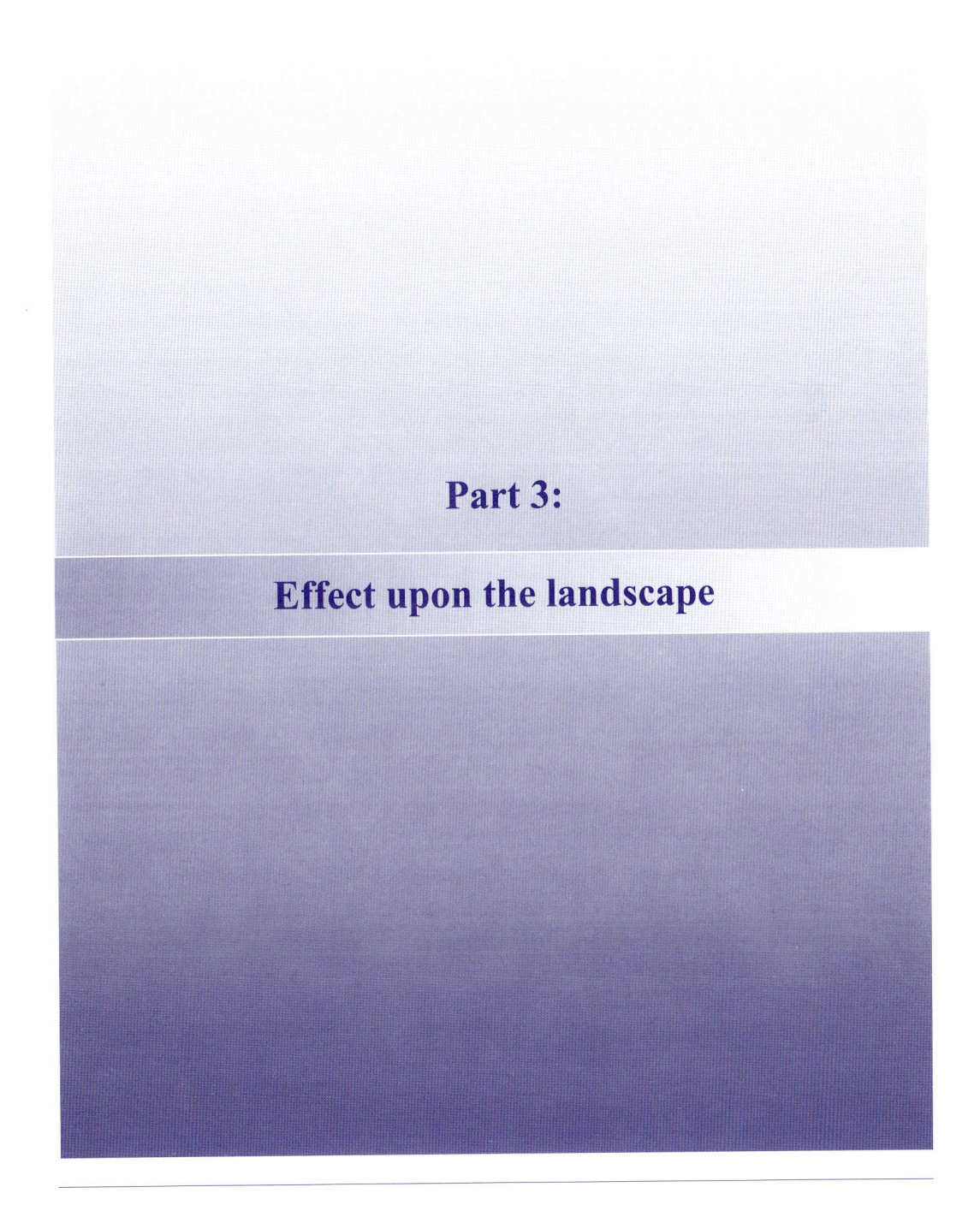

# Effect upon the landscape

# Farm and Factory: Revolution in the Borders

## Part 3: Effect upon the landscape

The landscape of the Borders has seen massive changes as a result of the agricultural and industrial changes of the 18th and 19th centuries. When Timothy Pont mapped the river valleys of the Borders in the 1580s the landscape was still organised to conform to a way of life which was still largely unchanged from medieval times.

For 6,000 years farming had encroached on the natural wild wood of the Borders and the only substantial stands of trees which still survived were in the valleys of the Jed, Ettrick and Yarrow Waters and lower Tweeddale (*see Early Settlers in the Borders*). Elsewhere trees survived where the ground they occupied was of no use to farmers, or where they were carefully coppiced as a source of fuel. The cultivated land that surrounded settlements of all sizes was worked communally in open fields. Individual land holdings were based on groups of three strips, nominally totalling twenty-two yards (20.1 metres or one chain) in width and two hundred and twenty yards (201 metres or one "furrow length" or furlong) in extent. Together a group of standard strips made up an area of 4,840 square yards or one acre (0.405 hectares). In practice, many strips, or ridges were narrower than this and could be significantly longer or shorter than a standard furlong.

These open fields had been tended for many generations and the plants which grew on them were strictly controlled. Beyond the common fields, areas which had been denuded of trees in the distant past had become moorland with a fauna and flora of their own, varying with the quality of the soil. Lochans, marshes and bogs existed in low-lying ground where the drainage was poor, although by the Middle Ages many of these had filled up naturally with dead vegetation which, in time, formed peat at places such as Gordon Moss, Whim Moss and Threepwood Moss (Melrose). Such places formed an important source of fish and waterfowl and reeds for thatch, mats or basketry.

In 1600 a wide range of vegetation covered the Borders countryside and the vast majority of plant species were of native origin. Cereal species, which had been introduced from the continent by 4,000BC and had their origins in the Near East, now enjoyed almost exclusive rights to those areas of land which were still under the plough. Herb species had been increased under the Roman imperial occupation and again by medieval monks, who may also have extended the range of tree species. Although the larger indigenous mammals were by this time extinct, newcomers such as the rabbit had been introduced in the medieval period (*see Early Settlers in the Borders and Christian Heritage in the Borders*).

Agricultural and industrial change had an impact, not only on the way in which the landscape was arranged, but how it was clothed and populated. The pre-improvement landscape was transformed in a relatively short space of time to be replaced with a countryside much like the one of today.

## Expansion and reorganisation of farmland

The remnants of the traditional open field system are best preserved in the Lammermuir Hills, the Cheviot foothills and parts of the Tweedsmuir Hills where arable farming was abandoned in place of stock rearing (**fig.16**). In such places as Lethem (Southdean: **Plate 10**) or around the Dirrington Laws (Greenlaw/ Longformacus) extensive systems of rig and furrow are now covered by moorland, while grazing animals suppress any growth of scrub over them. Redundant turf-banked stock enclosures that overlie former rigs at Lethem and Newcastleton date from the 18th and 19th centuries and are a powerful indication of the process which cleared the uplands of much of their population. On steep slopes the rigs sometimes took the form of cultivation terraces and good examples may be seen from the road at Romannobridge and Braemar Knowe (Morebattle).

# Farm and Factory: Revolution in the Borders

*Fig.16 An upland Borders farm. In the centuries before the Agricultural Revolution such farms would form the focus of a community of several families, but sheep herding replaced arable farming in the hills and required fewer employees, so many rural workers moved to the towns.*

Traces of the runrig system that still survive in lowland areas are usually where the land has either been removed from agricultural use or used for pasture. Rigs were only deliberately levelled where the ground continued in arable production. Where trees have been planted fragments of the earlier arable strips can frequently be found. One of the clearest examples of this type of survival is to be found on Melrose Golf Course, where the old rigs are now incorporated into the fairways and present an additional hazard to players.

## *Intake and drainage*

While upland owners found sheep and cattle more economic than arable cultivation, in the lowlands improving landowners sought to extend the available area of arable and bring additional land under the plough. Moorland was ploughed and marshes drained in the quest for greater productivity. This involved the construction of land drains to carry the excess water which were often on a substantial scale. These are revealed accidentally when they collapse under the weight of modern farm machinery. Such discoveries have long given rise to speculation as to their use, and improbable secret assignations or clandestine acts of devotion have been popular interpretations.

The barren mosses of Blairbog and Flowmossmuir (Newlands), tended only by a single herdsman, presented the third Duke of Argyll with a challenge. From 1729 he set out to reclaim the moor and turn it, not only into a fertile model farm, but an estate complete with mansion, pleasure gardens and dovecot. This was carried out at great expense, but the shortcomings of the soil eventually frustrated any hopes of reaping substantial returns from the land.

# Farm and Factory: Revolution in the Borders

## Soil improvement

One of the fundamental requirements for successful cultivation is good soil, but those of the Borders can vary from nutrient-rich to depleted soils in the space of a few miles. Huge sums were spent on the maintenance and improvement of soil fertility in the course of the 18th and 19th centuries.

Traditionally, animal dung was the main fertiliser used on farms across the country. Infields received dung naturally following the harvest when animals were allowed onto the stubble to graze. This was supplemented by manure from the fold yards after wintering of animals close to the farm buildings. The outfield received dung during summer months, when the animals were kept away from the growing crops of the infield. Whilst effective, this source of nutrients was limited by the number of animals available and only certain areas of a farm (the infield) would receive any useful amount of manure. Enclosure made it easier to concentrate animals and determine where they would deposit their dung, but the real breakthrough came with the use of lime to reduce the acidity of the soil.

Acid soils are characteristic of most of the Borders and their fertility is inferior to that of soils derived from limestone or other lime-rich rocks. By using burnt limestone or the lime-enriched clay known as marl to dress the surface of fields, farmers were able to neutralise enough of the acids in the soil to make a significant improvement in the productivity of their land. This involved a great deal of effort on the part of the farmer and 19th century accounts state that the quantities of shell marl required per acre varied between 25-30, 150-200 and 450-600 loads, according to the existing quality of the soil. At West Linton, where limestones occur naturally, soil in the outfield only required 20-24 *bolls* of "shells" in the 1790s. Although this method was employed widely in the Borders, it was particularly popular in Roxburghshire and Berwickshire where the majority of the cultivable land lay.

Wherever possible, marl was extracted locally from such places as Wester Lang Moss (now Lindean Reservoir: Selkirk: **Plate 11**) and Middlestots Bog (Edrom), but elsewhere it was necessary to bring in lime from outside the area.

***Fig.17*** *A 19th century limekiln at Deepsykehead, West Linton. Local limestone was burnt and added to farmland to reduce the acidity of the soil and improve fertility.*

**Plate 1** Midlem has retained its historic form for well over a thousand years. The houses are arranged around the village green and beyond their gardens the ghost of the medieval open field strips can be discerned in spite of 18th century enclosure.

**Plate 2** A 19th century designed landscape around Monteviot House, Ancrum.

**Plate 3** Newcastleton was developed by the Duke of Buccleuch in 1793 as a model village for weavers, who were brought together from different parts of the large parish of Castleton.

**Plate 4** Coldstream Bridge was built in 1763-66 by James Smeaton. Bridge tolls were paid at the tollhouse at the Scotland end, where marriages were also performed until 1856.

**Plate 5** The gravestone of Thomas Walker and family illustrates the level of child mortality in 19th century Galashiels. Betsy (3), Isabella (1), Robert (11) and Betsy (5) did not survive childhood - all died between 1836 and 1852.

**Plate 6** Ninewells Doocot, Chirnside. This 16th century "beehive" dovecote was a pigeon farm and provided a regular source of meat.

**Plate 7**  Greyfriars Garden, Jedburgh.  This garden incorporates the foundations of the medieval friary and has been planted with herbs and local varieties of fruit tree, for which Jedburgh was once famous.

**Plate 8**  The A1 and the East Coast Main Line railway enter Scotland along a narrow ledge between Lamberton Moor and the North Sea.  The turnpike along this stretch was completed in 1810, before which the route passed further inland.  The railway opened in 1846.

**Plate 9** Gunsgreen House & Doocot, Eyemouth. James Adam built this Palladian house for local merchant, James Nisbet in the period between 1753 and 1762. The cellars gave access to the adjacent harbour, which has been improved and extended since the 18th century.

**Plate 10** The Cheviot foothills at Lethem are marked with the parallel rigs of medieval cultivation. In places these are overlain by banked enclosures for the sheep and cattle that displaced the arable farmer in the 18th century.

**Plate 11** Lindean Reservoir was created in 1904 to provide water for nearby communities. Before that time it had been a quarry for marl to improve the fertility of farmland.

**Plate 12** Work on Mellerstain was started in 1725 for George Baillie by William Adam, who also laid out the grounds and dammed the River Eden. The house was completed by his son, Robert in 1778.

**Plate 13**  Roxburgh Viaduct was opened in 1851.

**Plate 14**  Cove Harbour survives substantially as it was when the breakwaters were completed in 1831, providing fishermen with a safe haven on the otherwise exposed Berwickshire coast.

**Plate 15** Walkerburn came into existence in the 1850s when a woollen mill was built beside the Walkers Burn. The mills were arranged along an artificial lade on the valley floor, the workers' houses clustered around them and the senior management houses stand detached amid landscaped gardens on the hillside. This is typical of the way in which the industrial towns of the Borders developed.

**Plate 16** Talla reservoir was built by the Edinburgh and District Water Trustees between 1895-1905. This massive undertaking required a special railway and an aqueduct tunnelled beneath the Tweedsmuir Hills.

In Berwickshire, for example, where there were few naturally occurring sources, lime was often bought and transported at great expense from Northumberland. John Spottiswoode of that Ilk spent over £40 in the mid-18th century on lime and similar or even greater amounts were being spent all over the country.

Lime and marl were not the only substances used in the mad race to improve the soil (**fig.17**). Many manures of differing homemade concoctions were mixed from such materials as animal horn, ashes and seaweed. During the mid 19th century it was found that bone was also an effective fertiliser and for a time the demand was so great that vast quantities were imported from Europe. Guano was also imported in vast quantities, initially from the North African coast and later from the guano islands of Peru and shipped to the fields of Britain.

Although not all of these measures were successful, the productivity of the soil did increase and the Lothians and Berwickshire in particular became some of the most prosperous and productive cereal producers in Scotland. The improving farmers also introduced crop rotation and favoured certain types of crop in particular to help improve the soil. At Newcastleton, for example, barley, rough bere, peas, oats, flax, potatoes and turnips were being grown in rotation by the 1790s. Elsewhere red clover was grown as hay, but also provided additional nitrogen for the soil.

Most of the land that was improved in the 18th and 19th centuries continues to be productive today. The main exceptions are areas which were brought into cultivation during the Napoleonic Wars (1797-1815) and during similar hostilities, to supply food which would otherwise have been imported. Such areas reverted to grazing once the need to cultivate them had passed. The success enjoyed by farmers in improving the quality of the soil, extending the arable land and introducing new crops had a lasting and immeasurable impact on the extent and distribution of cultivated and wild plant species and the animals that they support. Intake of new land, greater fertility and new crops were only the start of the change in the landscape. Social factors which resulted from them gave rise to the landscape which we see today.

## *Enclosure*

One of the reforming landowners of the 18th century was David Gavin and the Statistical Account (written c.1793) describes his improvements:

*"In 1758, Mr. Gavin purchased the estate, lying in the parishes of Langton, Dunse, and Longformacus. From that period till the time of his death in 1773, he was employed in the improvement of it. The plans he laid down were judicious, and the prosecution of them unremitted. The grounds were cleared of furze, and broom, and stones, and of every thing that could impede the operations of the plough. The rock marl, with which the estate abounds, and lime from the Northumberland hills, at the distance of 16 miles, were laid on as the soil required; the fields were divided with skill, and enclosed in the most substantial manner. In a short time, Langton assumed a most cultivated appearance, rewarded the attention, and repaid the expense the proprietor had bestowed upon it. The rent in 1758 was £1100; in 1773 it was let at upwards of £3000".*

Having extended and improved the arable, Gavin proceeded to enclose and plant the estate in the fashion of the day.

By the end of the 17th century landowners had started to restore trees and hedges to the countryside of the Borders. At this time most of the countryside was treeless, with the exception of Jed and Ettrick forests and relatively small areas of parkland around some of larger family seats, such as Branxholm (Hawick) and Wedderburn (Duns). The first changes were of limited effect; parklands were extended and new blocks of trees were planted,

# Farm and Factory: Revolution in the Borders

*Fig.18 A stell, or enclosure for corralling sheep. Such stone structures are characteristic of the Border hills and provided sheep with a wind break and farmers with a means of collecting scattered flocks.*

and occasionally the infields of the home or *mains* farm were enclosed.

The main changes came in the 18th century, when pioneers like Lord Kames and Lord Marchmont experimented with new crops such as potatoes and turnips (and were accounted "giddy-headed" by their neighbours) for it. They also paid attention to breeds of cattle and sheep and sought to improve them by introducing animals from England. Although Gavin's breeds of Merse and Lammermuir black cattle and Northumberland, Tweeddale and Lammermuir sheep were traditional local varieties, he was more interested in the productivity of his arable crops and kept fewer animals than he might "on account of the apprehended scarcity of fodder".

Effective development of mixed farming was severely restricted by the traditional open field system and individual landowners began to amalgamate smallholdings whenever the opportunity arose. The fields enclosed through these small-scale initiatives still retain the sinuous curves characteristic of the block of rigs that comprised them. Major landlords went much further, however and re-organised medieval strips and new intake into more manageable square fields and marked them out with stone dykes or post and rail fences, which they also planted with thorn hedges. As much of the newly won land was some distance from the village nucleus, new farms were built to allow farmers immediate access to it. Shelterbelts of trees were planted around farms and fields to reduce the effects of the wind and provide cover for game. Larger plantations provided standard trees for timber as well as roundwood for fencing and fuel.

After a few decades of growth the countryside had been transformed. The high demand for sheep had turned upland areas into vast pastures, which now included much former arable land as well as the deserted homes of displaced tenant farmers and cottars. What new building there was in these areas usually consisted of pens or stells for animals. Sometimes these were large, irregular clusters of units built on the sites of ancient settlements, so that they could re-use the stones from the old ramparts or houses. More frequently, and probably as part of an overall estate plan, the stells consisted of circular walled

*Fig.19* Cottages at Leitholm. Although many 18th century single storey cottages still survive in the Borders, many were heightened in the 19th century as a result of increased prosperity. The two-storey house in the foreground has a ground floor of dark whinstone and a later, upper floor of lighter sandstone.

enclosures of stone or turf with a single narrow entrance which could be closed off. An example of this kind of stell has been reconstructed at St Mary's Loch (Yarrow) and many other examples can be seen around the head of the Ettrick Valley (**fig.18**).

In the arable lowlands the lasting contrast was even greater. Stone dykes, or more commonly hedges, separated the fields and trees once more formed a common feature of the landscape. Designed landscapes require careful maintenance, however, and knowledge of woodland management had been largely forgotten as trees had disappeared from the landscape. Landowners had to learn afresh how to look after their plantations and the results of long-term neglect are now evident in former hedges which consist of closely set rows of beech trees or lines of irregularly clustered thorn trees. Excessive pruning has killed off many hedge plants, while others can no longer serve as an effective barrier to animals without the addition of a wire fence.

New plantations were normally protected from browsing animals by an enclosing bank, and these sometimes survive when the trees inside have long since been felled. Other old plantings have been enlarged or surrounded by later forestry and may only be distinguished by the species of tree which they contain. The greater number of trees has increased the ability of scrub to regenerate over ungrazed land and supplement the overall tree cover of the region. Many areas of woodland now exist through default and the lack of grazing animals to suppress self-seeded trees.

## *Houses and landscaping*

The process of enclosure often accompanied changes in the principal landlord's estate. Many country houses were built, or rebuilt in the course of the 18th century amid newly laid out parkland. At Marchmont and Mellerstain in Berwickshire the architect William Adam (died 1748) was responsible not only for the design of buildings, but also for architectural features in the landscape, such as follies, bridges and a canal (**Plate 12**). Much of the original design and planting of the parkland was probably also the work of Adam. At Langton, where between 1755 and 1793 the population grew from 290 to 435, David Gavin removed the existing village to a new site and renamed it Gavinton.

The oldest cottages that survive in the Borders may not date from much before 1700. Many of those which survive show signs of enlargement from one storey to two (**fig.19**). The frontage of a cottage recently incorporated into a new wall at the front of a housing development on the east end of the Main Street at Newstead has mouldings around the door and windows characteristic of the 17th century, when the village contained an unusually large number of stonemasons. Medieval hovels with walls of mud and wattle would all have been replaced during the period of improvement, but there was a shortage of lime in the Borders and some stone buildings are still held together with clay rather than lime mortar or cement.

In the 19th century explorers following in the wake of Mungo Park and others brought back exotic plants which became popular and formed the basis of specimen collections, so that no country house was complete without its *arboretum*. Interest in botany grew and the arboretum became an essential element of the gardens of the wealthier classes. Trees such as Douglas Fir and Wellingtonia Pine were brought from North America, Monkey-Puzzle from Chile and Eucalyptus from Australia (**fig.20**). A multitude of imported shrubs and herbs found their way into humbler gardens, sometimes with regrettable consequences. The invasive Rhododendron and Japanese Knotweed have spread and become out of control, while Giant Hogweed is not only a nuisance but also a definite health hazard. The vast majority of trees in the Borders today are non-native species, of which the most numerous is Sitka Spruce, a North American introduction which is grown as a crop in large commercial forests.

Tastes required that there were also animals to ornament these parks and landscaped gardens, and the native red squirrel was re-introduced to the Borders in the 18th and 19th centuries from England and Scandinavia. In 1892 the grey squirrel was introduced to Loch Long from North America and as a result now threatens the Borders population of red squirrels, with which it competes.

*Fig.20 Himalayan Balsam is one of many exotic imported plants which now grows wild in the Borders countryside.*

## Raw materials and energy

Man has exploited plants and animals in Britain for at least 500,000 years, and for that time has also used stone to make an increasingly wide range of objects. Stone has been used in building for more than 5,000 years, often when timber was not readily available. The qualities of metals were first explored in Britain more than 4,000 years ago, iron has been in common use for well over two millennia and the Roman army might have mined lead at West Linton in the 2nd century AD. In the Middle Ages all these were exploited and wool from sheep was particularly important as a source of foreign revenue.

Except where fragments of ancient woodlands survived, peat and perhaps cow dung would have formed the basic household fuels. Water, wind and draught animals were used to turn wheels in mills and gin houses and in parts of the Borders this continued to be the case even after the introduction of coal-fired steam engines.

Water was an important resource also, not only for drinking, but also for the washing process needed at various stages of mineral extraction and manufacture of goods. Spinning and weaving of home-produced wool were carried out by hand on spinning wheels and handlooms as a cottage industry.

## *Minerals*

Compared to other parts of Scotland, the Borders suffer from a shortage of economically viable and readily exploitable mineral resources. The majority of available resources is found in the north-west corner of the region around West Linton and includes deposits of limestone and coal. In addition the Borders has some small scale metal deposits, such as lead, which can found at Siller Holes (West Linton) and in the Manor Valley, copper at Elba (Abbey St Bathans) and gold at Glengaber Burn (Yarrow). Although these were exploited in earlier times, they were too small to have attracted substantial investment in the 18$^{th}$ or 19$^{th}$ centuries.

On the other hand, agricultural improvement and developing industry led to the active working of many of the coal, lime and other mineral deposits. Quarry pits, kilns and/ or clamps for the extraction and burning of lime-rich rock are residual landscape features at Robert's Linn (Hobkirk) and Larriston (Castleton), where commercial operations provided lime to farmers for the improvement of soil. These may have grown from earlier localised use, and *Lymekill hedge fells* is recorded on Timothy Pont's map of the late 16$^{th}$ century at the site of the later lime works at Robert's Linn. The remains of a solitary kiln beside the Powet Sike on Kirndean Farm (Castleton) is a reminder that farms and estates also processed lime for their own use. These quarries and the dumps and features associated with them provide habitats for a variety of plants, including Common Rockrose upon which the Northern Brown Argus butterfly breeds.

The 18$^{th}$ and 19$^{th}$ centuries also saw the opening of a number of coal mines and stone quarries. Although these were mainly in the West Linton area, particularly around Carlops and Harlaw Muir, the Old Statistical Account records that there was a great deal of prospecting going on in different parishes across the Borders, such as Mordington (Berwickshire) and Oxnam (Roxburghshire). Quarries were opened up throughout the Borders to provide *greywacke* for building dykes and enclosures, sandstone for house building and whinstone for road building. Although now mostly abandoned, open cast coal mining continues on Harlaw Muir and whinstone is extracted from Craighouse Quarry.

Extraction of sand and gravel for the building industry has re-shaped many lowland locations, especially in the river valleys. Clay extraction

*Fig.21 The mill lade at Innerleithen in 1990. The waters of the Leithen were diverted along this lade to drive woollen mills, Robert Smail's print works and electric turbines.*

for brick and tile manufacture has led to the drainage and removal of a number of wetland habitats, although the closure and abandonment of these factories has led to the recovery of some of these environments. A ruinous 19th century brick kiln still marks the site of the "Whitrigbog Tileworks" (Mertoun:**fig 5**).

## *Sources of Power*

Wind, water and draught animals were the traditional sources of motive power before the invention of methods which harnessed the forces of steam and electricity.

As early as the 12th century the Cistercian monks of Melrose constructed a *cauld* or dam across the Tweed and diverted its waters along a *lade* to drive the abbey corn mill and to flush out the monastic drains. More than sixty water-powered corn mills (about one per parish) are shown on the maps of the Borders that Timothy Pont drew up in the late 16th century. They were all situated beside streams and worked through the ability of a head of moving water to turn a paddled wheel and thereby drive machinery. The lade took river water to the mill, where it flowed under (undershot) or over (overshot) the wheel. The undershot wheel was the most common and was known to the Roman architect and engineer Vitruvius as early as 27BC but various improvements to the paddles increased its efficiency and by the late 19th century it was used to drive a variety of machines and was the basis of the Borders woollen mills (**fig.21**).

The historic cores of Galashiels and Hawick spilled over onto the haughs or water meadows beside the rivers Gala and Teviot to accommodate the first woollen mills (**fig.4**). When mapped by John Wood in 1824 the principal lade off the Gala Water was driving a line of nine mills. Moreover, the lasting environmental effect of this expansion was to shift the town centre of Galashiels onto a new site between the mill lade and the river. By the 1830s the strain which this imposed on the water supply caused local manufacturers to industrialise the Ettrick haughs at Selkirk. By the 1860s it was noted that the low level of the Gala Water and its pollution by domestic effluent, particularly in dry summers, had

*Fig.22 A 19th century gin house at St Boswells. The circular open structure contained a revolving post which was turned by a horse and geared to machinery in the adjacent threshing barn. Farmers resorted to horse power when water power was unavailable.*

become a severe health hazard that was only alleviated by improved sewerage and water supply.

There were few windmills in the Borders, largely because most parts of the region were well suited to water power, and those which did exist were mostly in the low-lying Merse. Of those few that still exist, the windmill at Gunsgreenhill (Ayton) is the best preserved. They did not require caulds, lades or mill ponds and in consequence had little impact upon the environment, other than as a visual addition to the landscape. Wind power has recently been re-introduced at Soutra Hill where an extensive windfarm has been built in the interests of sustainable power. Although views differ as to the manner in which this has impacted upon the landscape, there has not yet been sufficient time to judge its impact, if any, upon the natural environment.

Draught animals pulled wagons, carts and ploughs and worked gins to drive threshing machines and other agricultural equipment such as butter churns. The reversed 'S' curves which are typical of the older types of rig and furrow were produced by draught teams of oxen as they turned the plough at the end of each furlong. The polygonal buildings where they turned the rotary gin were normally attached to threshing barns and several survive in the region, the mills at Ninewar and Clarabad Farms (Duns and Hutton respectively: **fig.22**) being particularly well-preserved examples. Both of these buildings are more or less intact and have their machinery still in place. The need for farms to keep draught animals, even when the main interest was in growing plants, has meant that areas of unploughed pasture have survived close to farm steadings and these often retain pre-enclosure rig and furrow which would otherwise have been leveled in cultivation.

The introduction of steam power in the late 18th century saw the demise of traditional sources of energy. Steam driven railway locomotives brought cheaper coal into the region from the 1840s, which made the use of steam more economical in the factories. New steam-driven mills were much larger than their water-driven predecessors and came to dominate the townscapes of Hawick, Galashiels and Selkirk.

The new energy source was also applied to agriculture. Mobile traction engines were used to pull ploughs and static engines were set up in farm steadings where they drove threshing machines and other equipment. The economic advantage of steam was particularly appreciated in Berwickshire where the tall chimneys needed to dispel the smoke from the boilers are still a characteristic of the Merse. Notable examples survive at Brieryhill and Broomdykes (Duns and Edrom respectively).

Gas lighting was first employed in London at the turn of the 19th century to light the Lyceum Theatre and the technology was subsequently adopted by industrialists to illuminate factories and mills and country landowners to light their homes. Sir Walter Scott lit his new house of Abbotsford with gas in the 1820s and a pipe from the equipment is still preserved in the house grounds. As the 19th century progressed gas was increasingly used to light streets and a wider range of domestic dwellings. and to provide this, gas companies were set up in the towns and villages. The atmosphere around these was usually tainted with the smell of escaping gas from the retorts which extracted the vapour from coal. Natural gas replaced coal or town gas for domestic use in the 1960s and most gasometers (gas storage tanks) have now been removed. One of the smallest municipal gasometers in Britain was located at Duns, but at Biggar, just beyond the western boundary of Scottish Borders, a small gasometer has been preserved as an ancient monument and is open to the public. Although gas is still used for domestic heating and cooking, it has long since been replaced by electricity as a source of light.

As a form of power, electricity was first produced by batteries and from the 1870s by dynamos driven by steam or water. Its earliest practical use came with the railways in the 1840s, when the electric telegraph conveyed messages (telegrams) along raised wires supported by poles. From about 1918 the telephone superseded telegrams and led to a further proliferation of telegraph poles.

Although Cragside in Northumberland, the home of inventor Sir William Armstrong, was the first house in Britain to be lit by electric light (1880), only one fifth of the homes in Britain were lit by electricity by the 1920s. In the 20th century the National Grid brought electricity to the Borders from coal-fired power stations outside the region and lines of cables and pylons criss-cross the countryside as a result. At Innerleithen and Walkerburn, however, water was used instead to drive turbines and produce *hydro-electricity* for textile mills. A large concrete tank in which water was collected for the Walkerburn turbine still stands on the summit of Kirnie Law (Innerleithen).

## *Water Supply*

The problem of providing clean water for drinking and washing increased in proportion to population growth. As the rural population actually decreased, those remaining found no particular problem in meeting their own needs, although some pond digging may have been carried out in the Merse to provide all-year round drinking water for animals. In the towns the inadequacy of wells and the danger of contamination from sewage through percolating ground water led to the establishment of private water companies. As a result of the 19th century Police Acts local communities were able to develop civic water supplies and in the later part of that century many small reservoirs were built to supply the settlements.

In 1844 a company was formed to provide water for Peebles, but after a number of problems the company's assets were taken over by the Town Council in 1863. The Council developed a new supply from a small reservoir which, though disused and grassed over, can still be seen beside the Meldon Burn (Lyne). This too was inadequate and a new source was established in the Manor Valley which now passes through a filter bed with a capacity of 1,818,400 litres (400,000 gallons).

In 1904 the South East Scotland Water Board constructed a reservoir of 227,300,000 litres (50 million gallons) at Lindean to serve customers in Newtown, Midlem, St Boswells and Lilliesleaf. By 1972 alternative water supplies were available from the much larger Alemoor Reservoir (Roberton) and the site has since been developed as a nature reserve.

The higher rainfall and topography of the Tweedsmuir Hills was one of the factors behind the building of Talla Reservoir (Tweedsmuir) to supply water by gravity to the City of Edinburgh. Work started in 1895 by the Edinburgh and District Water Trust and took ten years to complete. After the Second World War the Fruid Reservoir (Tweedsmuir) added its water to that of Talla, and in 1983 the Megget Reservoir (Yarrow) was opened to meet increased demand in Lothians.

# Part 4:

# Surviving archaeological features

## Part 4: Surviving archaeological features

Visitors to the Borders have a real opportunity to explore places where the effects of the Industrial and Agricultural Revolutions were profound. Many of the largest settlements in the Borders owe their growth to the rise of the textile industry and many of the farms which dot the landscape were formed as a result of the events described in this book. Although few of the factories are accessible, many of the buildings are visible in the urban landscape and some of the local museums hold displays on the industrial heritage of the area. Additionally many other industrial features are still prominent in the Borders landscape and the visitor may still find tollhouses, disused railways and associated buildings, bridges and harbours, as well as old quarries and mines.

The countryside through which the visitor travels holds many remains connected with this time, such as post-improvement farmsteads and cottages, abandoned farms, doocots, chimneys, windpumps and estate villages. Although there are only limited opportunities to visit and examine these features at close range, travelling through the Borders countryside affords the visitor the chance to identify many of the features described within this book.

## Transport remains

### Land

The Agricultural and Industrial Revolutions were periods of great change for the transport network of Britain as a whole and this change had a profound effect on the Borders. Before the network was developed and upgraded, modes of travel and the condition of roads were fairly primitive. Roads were no more than dirt tracks defined by the passage of people and animals. Remnant sections of Dere Street and other Roman roads were virtually the only places where thought had been put into road building. Bridges were scarce and fords were widely used, for example between Melrose and Gattonside.

The most visible structures of the revolution in the transport network, both road and railway are bridges (**fig.23**). One of the earliest examples was across the Tweed at Peebles. The core of this stone bridge is thought to date to the 15$^{th}$ century when it was built to replace an earlier wooden bridge. The bridge comprises five segmental arches, with the medieval core near the middle of the central arch, which may have been constructed by John of Peebles, who was also responsible for the construction of the Tay Bridge at Perth. It was originally c.2.4m (8ft) wide and enlarged in 1834 to 6.4m (21ft) for an estimated cost of £1,000. There are plaques on the inner and outer sides of the western parapet in commemoration. The bridge was further widened on the east side by the Town Council between 1897 and 1900 for the cost of £8,000 and it is this bridge which is in use today. From below it is possible to trace some of the earlier arches. It is still an impressive bridge, faced with whinstone and sandstone dressings and ornamented with cast-iron lamps with entwined dolphins which stand on the piers.

With the Union of the Crowns and the subsequent Act of Union there was a greater need for better links between Scotland and England. One of the first routes to be improved as a result was the east coast route known as the "Great North Road" in preparation for the journey of King James VI from London to Edinburgh in 1617. The most spectacular of these improvements was the construction of a bridge across the Tweed at Berwick. Construction on this bridge commenced in 1611 and continued until 1634, thus missing the King's visit by 17 years. It was hoped that the bridge would be seen as a symbol of unification of the two kingdoms and it was a suitably impressive structure to reflect this. The fifteen span, 355m (1165ft), red sandstone construction which still stands today, although now dwarfed

*Fig.23* Kelso Bridge was designed by John Rennie and opened in 1803 as toll bridge. Rennie combined elegance with the world's first use of elliptical arches and subsequently employed them in his design for London Bridge.

by the Royal Tweed and Royal Border Bridges, is a fitting monument to this ideal. Further improvements were made to this route in the following centuries, including a massive deviation in the form of a turnpike. One of the most impressive later features is the Pease Bridge (Cockburnspath). This is a fine four arch brick built bridge standing 40m (130ft) high over the Pease Dean. When it was opened in 1786 this was the tallest bridge in the world.

The impetus to upgrade the road network arose, in part, from the need to import materials such as lime to enhance the quality of the land and by the late 18th century road improvements had reached their peak with the foundation of Turnpike Trusts. The road network, which serves the Borders today, is largely a result of the work carried out by these trusts. By obtaining permission from parliament, roads could be constructed and improved, bridges built, and most importantly for the trustees, tolls could be levied. The trustees used the money from the tolls to recoup their expenditure on the creation of the turnpikes.

Closely associated with turnpike roads were tollhouses. These buildings were an integral part of any turnpike road and the toll bar which accompanied them was, in fact, where the name turnpike was derived. The bars were simply wooden poles which stretched across the road and lifted or pivoted when the toll had been paid. No toll bar now survives but a few have left their mark on the landscape in another form, as place names such as Carter Bar (Jedburgh) highlight. Although tollhouses came in various shapes and sizes they all had certain features in common. They were often based on a normal house with either windows at either side or a projected front porch with side windows, so that there were views along the road in both directions. Few examples now survive, as many were situated immediately beside the turnpike and were vulnerable to demolition in the course of later road widening. Those few that have survived have been modified, extended or converted into other uses, these include the "Marriage House" at Coldstream Bridge, Greenbank Toll (Roberton) and Birkenside (Legerwood).

Bridges are, however, the most common features of the improvements in the road network that are still visible in the landscape. Several still stand close to modern roads where they have been isolated or abandoned as a result of later road improvements. The bridges at Cleikemin (c.1782: Ancrum), and Leaderfoot (1779-80) are fine examples of small turnpike bridges, both built to service the road north to Edinburgh from Jedburgh. Larger bridges were also constructed notably at Coldstream (1763-6) and Mertoun (1841) both of which span the Tweed. Unlike the concrete road bridges that are a familiar sight today these bridges were built with local stone and often adorned with carvings and other decoration. The bridge at Leaderfoot is a particularly good example of a finely decorated bridge which, although now closed to motorised traffic, is part of the Tweed Cycleway and accessible to the visitor. The Leaderfoot (or more properly Drygrange) bridge is an elegant three arched sandstone bridge with carved stone urns set into niches on either side of the central arch. The Drygrange bridge was not the first (nor the last) bridge to be built in this location; almost 2,000 years earlier the Roman army built a bridge here as part of their military road from York to Perthshire. No trace remains of this bridge but it is likely to have been situated a short distance downstream. Two other bridges cross the Tweed at Leaderfoot. The more modern is a concrete road bridge and carries the A68 trunk road. The most eye-catching of the bridges here, however, was never used for road transport, but rather reflects a different innovation in the improvement of communications. This is the Leaderfoot Viaduct. One of the most impressive sights in the Borders, this red sandstone railway bridge, which was built for the Berwickshire Railway in 1865, comprises thirteen arches, the tallest measuring some 37m (121ft) above the Tweed. Extra buttresses have been added to the southernmost piers for strength.

Some bridges constructed to accommodate the new turnpikes are still in use as road bridges. Two fine examples are Lowood or 'Bottle' Bridge (1762: Melrose) and Yair Bridge (1760: Selkirk). The former was on the turnpike from Galashiels to Newstead whilst the latter was part of the turnpike from Selkirk to Edinburgh.

Not all bridges in the Borders were of the standard stone construction; a few iron suspension bridges were also constructed. The largest of these is the Union Suspension Bridge. Built by Capt. Sir Samuel Brown, with advice from John Rennie in 1819-20, it was the first large suspension bridge in Britain. The bridge is little altered from the original, other than some strengthening which was undertaken at the beginning of the 20$^{th}$ century. This 5.5m (18ft) wide, 112m (368ft) long bridge has a timber carriageway suspended 8m (27ft) above the Tweed by three pairs of swept, wrought iron cables with iron bolt brackets (invented by Capt. Brown) linking iron suspenders. At either end, of the bridge is a large pink sandstone pylon, both of which are adorned with a plaque bearing the motto "*VIS UNITA FORTIOR 1820*", or "stronger united". To the west of the bridge (on the Scottish side) stood the Union Bridge Tollhouse which has now been converted into a private dwelling.

The 19$^{th}$ century brought a further improvement in the transport network with the arrival of the railway into the Borders. In 1844 Parliament granted approval for the first cross-border railway line to run from Edinburgh to Berwick along the East Coast and this was opened in June 1846. During the course of the next sixty years every town in the Borders was linked to the rail network (**fig.24**). The construction of this network added many new features to the landscape of the Borders such as bridges and viaducts, track beds and stations and also changed the landscape through which the railways passed.

With the exception of the disused track beds and a collection of bridges and viaducts, there are few surviving structures connected with the Border railways. On the former Waverley Route

*Farm and Factory: Revolution in the Borders*

## Railways in the Borders

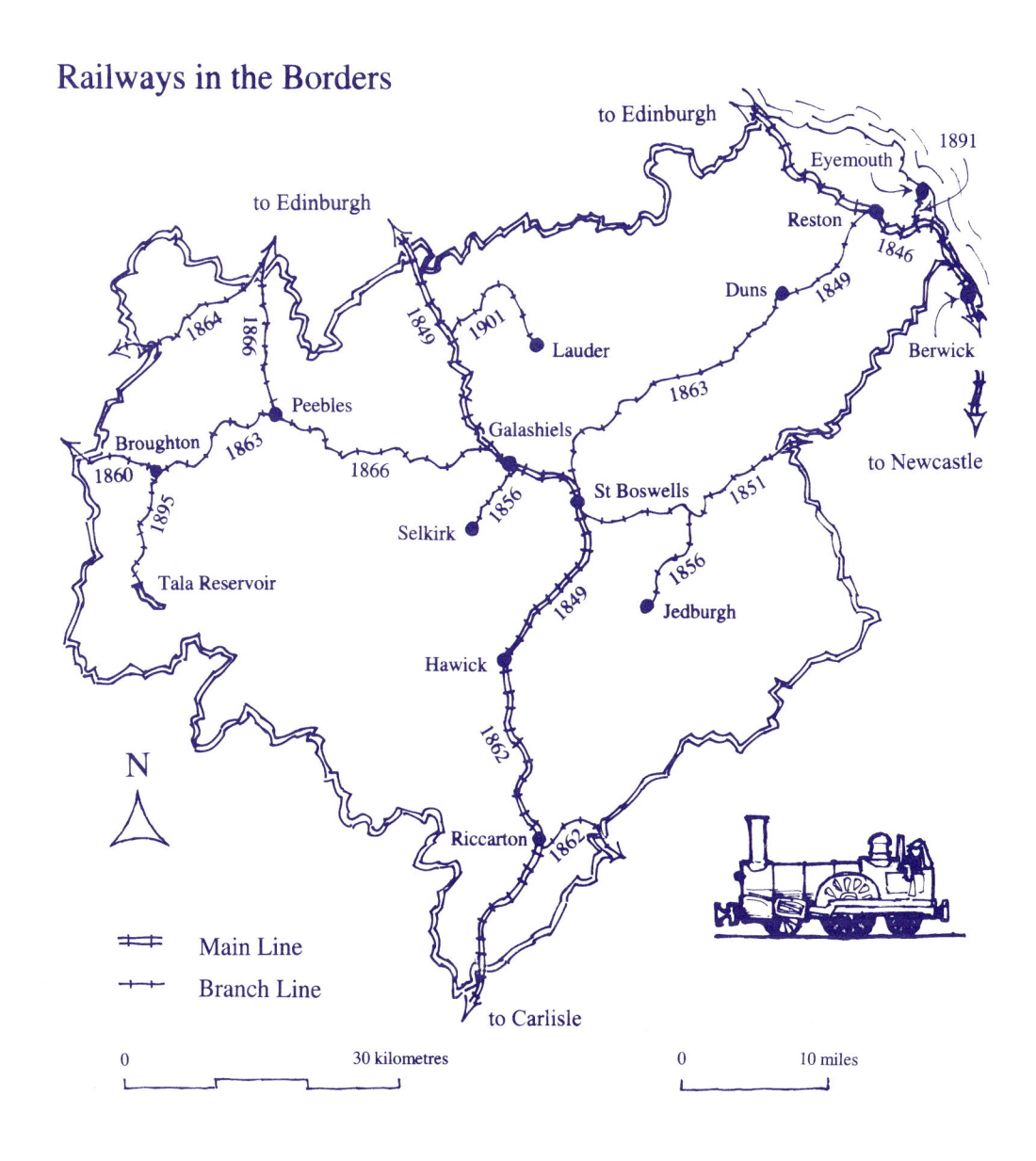

*Fig.24 Railways provided faster travel than ever before and "railway mania" led to the construction of lines throughout Britain. Different sections of the Borders network are shown here with their opening dates. By 1970 only the coastal Edinburgh to Newcastle line survived.*

61

from Edinburgh to Carlisle, the line can be traced along the Gala Water but all that remains of the former Galashiels Station is the cutting revetment beside Ladhope Vale and the road bridge over Currie Road. The Tweed Bridge and old track bed beyond (the "Black Path") is now a footpath, and the line has been used for a substantial length of the Melrose Bypass, beside which the former Melrose Station stands in a splendid state of preservation. Further south, the Stations of St Boswells Junction and Hawick have been obliterated, but cuttings and embankments still preserve the line. The finest monument on the line is Shankend Viaduct (Cavers), beyond which is a signal box. The end of Whitrope Tunnel and some ancillary works still survive beside the B6399 before the route reaches Riccarton Junction and drops into Liddesdale.

Elsewhere, some lengths of track bed have been converted to use as footpaths, for instance beside the Tweed at Peebles, although most are on private land and not accessible. Stretches of other former lines can still be seen beside the River Tweed in upper Tweeddale and between Galashiels and Peebles and beside the Teviot at Roxburgh.

The most impressive surviving features connected to the railway network are undoubtedly the bridges and viaducts which were needed to traverse some of the Border valleys. In addition to Shankend and Leaderfoot viaducts (described above: **Plate 13**) other impressive rail bridges exist at Roxburgh, Neidpath (Peebles) and Dunglass. Although not as tall as that at Leaderfoot, the fourteen span Roxburgh Viaduct is another fine example of railway architecture and was built in 1850 for the Northern British Railway. The viaduct stands 22m (72ft) above the River Teviot and the four central northern piers have extended bases which carry a wrought-iron truss bridge for pedestrian use. The six span viaduct at Dunglass is one of a few original rail bridges that are still in use on the East Coast Main Line.

Although there were a large variety of buildings associated with the railway including station houses and buildings, signal boxes, wagon sheds and generator buildings very few have survived. A few of the former station houses have been converted to serve as private homes, including those at Innerleithen, Roxburgh and Stobo.

## *Sea*

Prior to the 18$^{th}$ century there was little need for work to be carried out to improve any of the natural harbours or landing places along the coast. However, after the Union of 1707 an increase in trade created a need for more substantial harbours for handling fish and traded goods. Although work was carried out to improve the facilities at Eyemouth and Cove, these early works were removed in the 19$^{th}$ century to make way for more extensive harbour works. Work was also carried out at Burnmouth and St Abbs in the late 1820s and early 1830s.

At Burnmouth the "boat harbour" was enlarged in 1879 with further works in the mid 20$^{th}$ century. The earliest works were L-shaped in plan with a pier 52m (170ft) long with a parapet and walkway. A later pier was constructed to enclose the harbour and there was a later extension to the main pier. The existing harbour works at Cove were completed in 1831 and consist of two piers, a northern one which extends south-east and southern one with extends northwards to form an enclosed harbour of just over 1.2ha (3 acres: **Plate 14**). To the east of the southern pier, cut into the cliff face are two flights of step-like edges which probably represent the remains of two earlier attempts in the 1750s and 1820s to establish a harbour here. Both these attempts were met with failure when storms destroyed the workings. The most interesting feature at Cove is not the harbour itself, but is an access tunnel that is cut through the cliff on the west side of the bay and which contains a system of cellars cut into the rock.

The third small harbour to be upgraded in the

1830s was St Abbs. Work began in 1831 to provide a refuge for fishing boats and a developed version of this still exists, within larger, more recent works. The original harbour was roughly square, only extending to cover an area of 0.1ha (0.25 acre) inside a natural basin amongst the littoral rocks. The harbour has since been extended outwards to enlarge the harbour and provide extra shelter. The site is now part of St Abbs Voluntary Marine Reserve and is a favourite spot for divers.

The main port in the Borders is Eyemouth, located at the outflow of the Eye Water, but as late as the 18th century its facilities were suitable only for fishing boats. At the river's mouth a stone pier was built on the right bank, under the advice of John Smeaton in 1768. This complimented another pier that had been built on the left bank shortly before 1750. The quarrying work required to construct Smeaton's pier also enlarged the harbour and a maximum depth of 6m (20ft) was obtained. Although more recent works have completely altered the approach to the port from the sea and the harbour was enlarged between 1996-2000, parts of the 18th century piers are still recognisable in the fabric.

One of the most prominent features of the development of Eyemouth harbour is the imposing Gunsgreen House. The house was designed and built for James Nisbet, a local merchant, by James Adam sometime between 1753 and 1762. It is located directly above the harbour and still dominates the view over the harbour from the town. It is built in a hollow which has been excavated from the hillside behind it, thus providing shelter in an extremely exposed location. Integral to the overall composition of this grand town house is the large, rubble-built bastion which acts as a forecourt for the building. Its wall projects as a segmental bow towards the harbour, reinforced by eight pyramidal buttresses with blank windows set in the spaces between and topped by a battlement. Beneath the house and accessed via the base of the bastion are a series of barrel vaulted cellars which were probably constructed for James Nisbet's mercantile interests. As a whole this is a fine example of a merchant's house and unique in the Borders.

In addition to the harbours, other features, such as lighthouses, coastguard stations and boatyards were also constructed during the 18th and 19th centuries. Situated on the stunning cliffs at St Abbs Head is the only lighthouse in the Borders. The lighthouse was designed by David and Thomas Stevenson and opened in 1862. It replaced an earlier signal station, also for shipping, which was established in 1826 (to replace an even earlier structure). The site of the earlier signal station is situated adjacent to a modern car park and some remains still survive. The earliest structure is represented by a grass covered two-roomed rectangular structure; the remains of the 1826 signal station are by a modern indicator board and to the west of this are the remains of a pump which supplied the site with water. Later coastguard cottages and garden (built 1907) are also present on the site.

The lighthouse is a single storey structure with a small but powerful light within. To the north-east of the lighthouse sits a foghorn on top of a semicircular plan block. A single storey lightkeeper's cottage sits a short distance from the lighthouse with two other cottages; the Lighthouse Retreat and Keeper's Hold. Although the lighthouse is now fully automated and the cottages are holiday homes this group is an important feature of the Borders maritime past.

## Agricultural remains

A wide range of buildings associated with the Agricultural Revolution and its effects are visible in the Borders landscape. The most commonly viewed are perhaps the isolated lines of cottages, built for farm workers beside many country roads. Equally common are farms, often set back from the road but still clearly visible.

# Farm and Factory: Revolution in the Borders

With closer inspection, however, a visitor to the Borders is able to identify many other features such as solitary doocots standing abandoned in fields, chimneys (especially in Berwickshire) that were once attached to engine houses that held cunning devices, which powered farm machinery. The visitor will pass through designed landscapes, once completely enclosed but now invaded by modern roads and while passing through these, glimpses may be gained of the country houses that sat proudly within them. Perhaps less obvious, but still visible are water features such as mill lades, dams and ponds all formerly used to power agricultural machinery.

## Rural landscape

Pre-enclosure farmsteads were fairly basic and normally included a long, single storey farmhouse, which in many cases accommodated people in one half and animals in the other. Farm produce, particularly grain, would have been stored close by in a separate barn. The open area between these buildings would have contained stacks of straw or hay as well as the midden where kitchen waste and dung, human and animal, were put for transfer to the arable fields as fertilizer. Fruit and vegetables would have been grown in a small garden attached to the rear of the house. There are no upstanding examples of this type of steading left in the Borders, although many survive as turf covered foundations, for example by Smailholm Tower. At Laidlawstiel (Caddonfoot) cultivation terraces and rig are associated with the medieval farmstead.

The Agricultural Revolution not only brought about great changes in the way farming operated but also in the layout of farms themselves. One of the first changes was the formalisation of the layout of the farm. The buildings would be grouped around three sides of a courtyard in a flattened U-shape, with the farmhouse occupying a central position opposite the open end of the courtyard. The stack yard, where the corn was stored before threshing, lay outside the courtyard to the west of the barn so that the sheaves got plenty of air and did not rot. Inside the courtyard cattle could be fed during the winter. A line of cart sheds faced into the yard, the number of arches being a good measure of the size of the farm. Above them were granaries with the threshing barn built on at right angles at the rear. Early ranges of outbuildings often formed three sides of a courtyard with a wall on the fourth but later designs filled in the fourth side with another range of buildings pierced by an entrance, sometimes with a high-arched gateway. Examples of 18th century farmsteadings survive, usually with later alterations, for instance, at Blackadder Mount (1785).

As farms adjusted to increased production the location of the farmhouse was frequently moved away from the steading. This also suited the new social position which agricultural wealth brought. Elegant two- or three-storey detached buildings, far from the midden, now emphasised the social distance between the farmer and his workers. In the eastern Borders and particularly in the Merse, the new farmhouses were often roofed with imported slate while outbuildings and farm workers' cottages were covered in red pantiles which were cheaper and became the standard replacement for straw thatch. Farmsteads in the uplands had more limited storage requirements with correspondingly fewer buildings.

Most of the farmsteads which can be seen today date from the 1820s to the 1850s. These later steadings were architect-designed, often from widely circulated pattern books. Although laid out on even more strictly functional lines than their predecessors, they were often more finely embellished, especially estate farms. They were built during a period when farming had reached a peak of prosperity and farmers and landowners alike were prepared to spend a lot of money in improving the look of their farmsteads. Decorations included clock towers for instance

## Farm and Factory: Revolution in the Borders

at Blackadder Mount, Ladykirk and Newton Don (Nenthorn) and dovecots, for instance at Edrom Newton (above the entrance gate) while the architectural styles used varied from the severely Classical, through Scots Baronial to Gothic Revival.

Lugate Farm (Stow: **fig.25**) is an example of the development of a hill farm. It is situated on the west side of the valley of the Lugate Water, a tributary of the Gala, is bounded on the north by the Gately Burn and on the south straddles the Hope Burn. The Fore Burn and Back Burn flow into the Fowie Burn and drain the central part of the farm. The holding was surveyed in 1809 by John Leslie and covered 770ha (1,740 acres).

There is documentary reference to Lugate in 1543-4 and in 1593 there was a "tower and manor" there. General Roy's map of 1752-4 indicates "Lugart" on the site of the present farm and "Lugart Old Castle" on the opposite side of the Lugate Water and a mile or so upstream. From the Second Statistical Account and from Leslie's survey, it seems probable that "Luggate Castle" was the tower of 1593 and was located where the remains of "Ewes Castle" lie today. The farmhouse and steading of "Luggate", which incorporated an older structure, is identified with the manor of 1593.

In 1809 137.7ha (340 acres) of the farm were arable, 40.9ha (101 acres) were meadow, 524.5ha (1,295 acres) were pasture and 1.2ha (3 acres) were woodland. Of the arable, 3.2ha

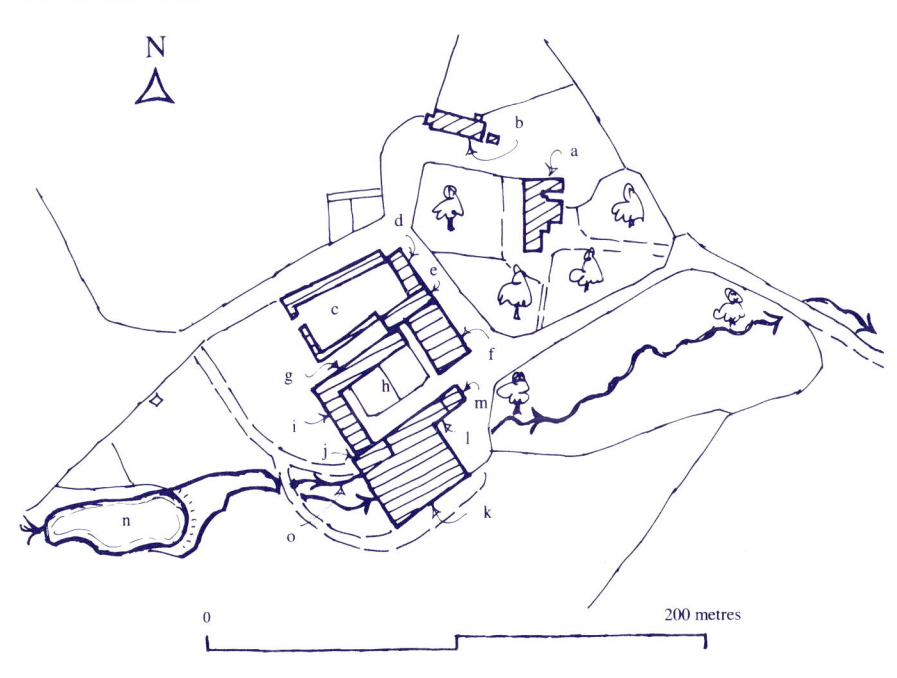

*Fig.25 A Borders hill farm (Lugate, near Stow). The buildings were almost all erected in the 19$^{th}$ century, but in 1950 the various elements had the following functions: (a) farm house; (b) kennels, feed store, trap park, feed store; (c) stack yard for corn; (d) shed for four carts; (e) turnip shed; (f) and (g) loose boxes; (h) open cattle shed; (i) cart horse stable; (j) threshing mill; (k) cattle shed run as dairy; (l) wash room for dairy; (m) bothy for seasonal workers; (n) mill pond; (o) mill lade.*

(8 acres) were identified as turnips and 10.5ha (26 acres) as "enclosed corn park" and 26.3ha (65 acres) as "oatfield". The crops in the remaining arable are not identified. Two isolated buildings stood in pasture on opposite sides of Back Burn; Micklehoperigg was a shooting lodge and Fowie a shepherd's cottage. The 1.2ha (3 acres) of woodland indicated in 1809 were shared between two plantations in pasture on the northern part of the farm and were probably game coverts related to the shooting lodge.

By the time of the 1st Edition Ordnance Survey 1:10,560 map, drawn between 1862 and 1884, the remains of the manor house were still visible to the north of a new farmhouse. Various outbuildings had been extended or rebuilt and the waters of the Hope Burn had been dammed to drive a threshing mill. An additional 22.3ha (55 acres) of hill pasture and meadow had been enclosed as arable to bring the total to 160ha (395 acres).

By the time of the 2nd Edition OS 1:2,500 map of 1907 the farmhouse had been extended and the grounds improved by diverting farm traffic around its southern side. The steading had been extended over the Hope Burn by the construction of a large cattle shed and a settling pond had been dug upstream from the mill pond, possibly to collect silt. This might have been in response to run off from ploughed fields as a result of a massive expansion of the arable, which by this time had more than doubled to approximately 344.3ha (850 acres). Thousands of trees had been planted in long strips along ridges west of the farm and more were added in the later 20th century.

In 1950 the farm included the following: farm house, with dairy attached; kennels; sheds for horses, trap and feed; loose boxes for dairy cows; feed store; tool store; turnip shed; saw mill; stables for cart horses; feed bruiser house; straw shed; threshing mill; cattle shed (used as a dairy) with grain store above; open cattle shed with additional loose boxes; washing up area; stack yard; shed for four carts; bothy for seasonal Irish labourers; foreman's house.

Since 1950 the pasture has been sold off and increased mechanisation is reflected in the purchase of tractors, the addition of a trailer shed, additional cattle shed and grain drier in the 1960s and a silage pit and cattle shed for 160 suckler cows in the 1970s.

Many of the estates of the wealthy country landowners, such as Floors and Mellerstain, derived a significant part of their income directly from farming. Although they were organised as farms and worked on a large scale, they also placed a great deal of emphasis on the comfort and prestige of the owner. Manderston is situated 2km (1.5 miles) east of Duns in the fertile area of the Borders known as the Merse (**fig.26**). This large country house sits within a designed landscape and has its own estate farm, known as Buxley, which would include many of the functional features already noted at Lugate. Although there has been a house and a park at Manderston at least as early as the 16th century when it was recorded by Timothy Pont, very little is known of this property. By the mid 18th century, there was a house surrounded by a formal landscape and approached by a long avenue. This house was cleared away and Dalhousie Weatherstone constructed the present building when General Maitland may have owned it. The property was bought by Robert Miller (in 1850) and then passed to his brother, Sir William, in 1880. Sir William had made his fortune trading with the Russians during the Crimean War and had been recently created a baronet. He carried out some additions to the house including a large Renaissance roof, although it was his second son, James, who undertook the majority of the rebuilding works. Sir James and his wife also carried out a programme of improvements to the grounds, including the boathouse, stables and Home Farm. Sir James then went on to commission the architect John Kinross to enlarge the house, which involved adding a new wing and servants' court and refurbished the interior.

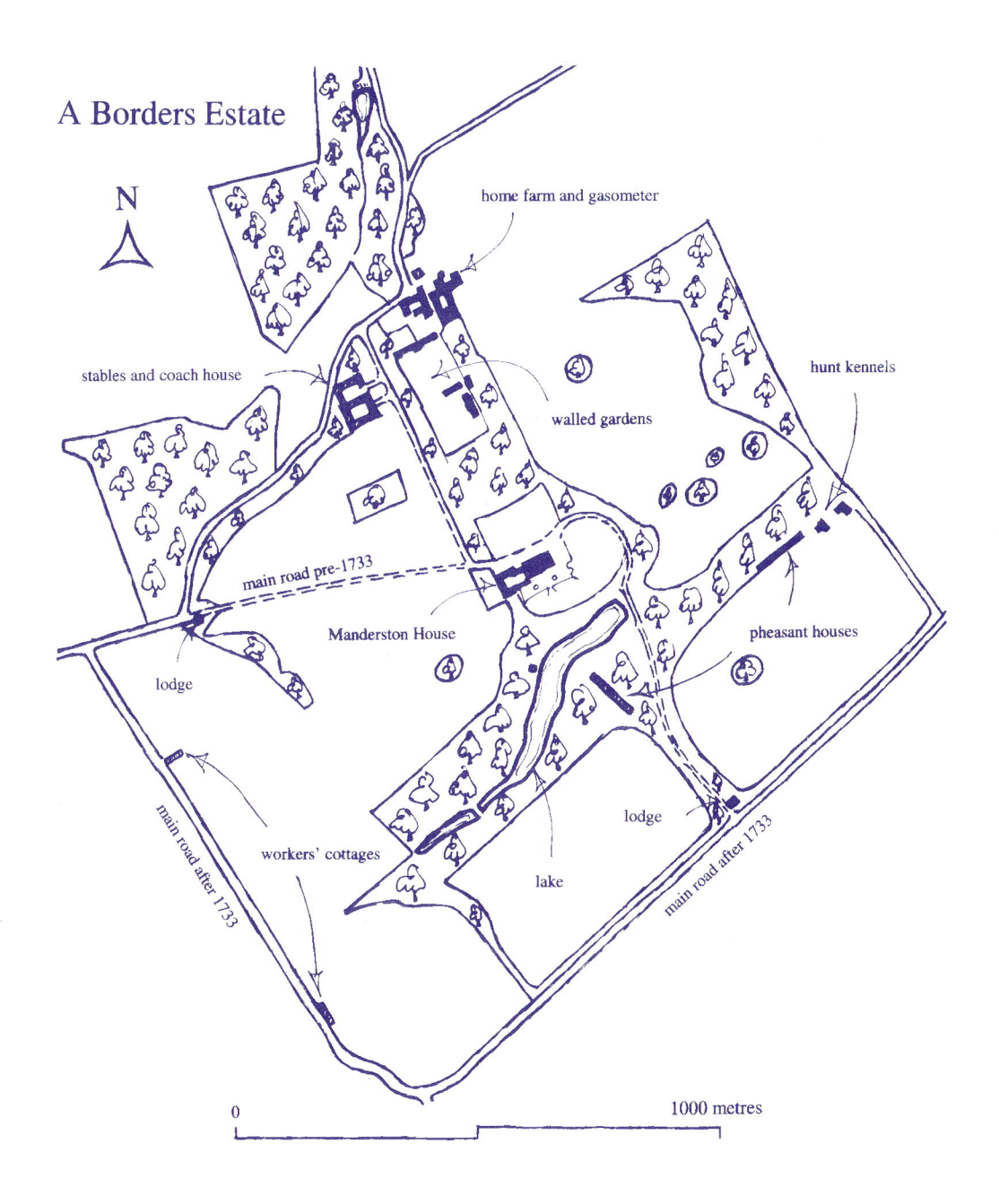

***Fig.26*** *The central elements of a large Borders estate are well represented at Manderston, Edrom. The elements of an ordinary farm, including agricultural buildings, house, stables and garden are all present, but on a huge scale and set within a landscape that includes a park with lake, gatekeeper's lodges, workers' cottages, hunt kennels and pheasant houses. Diversion of the public road to avoid the house is a reflection of the owner's influence in the 18$^{th}$ century.*

# Farm and Factory: Revolution in the Borders

Several components now comprise the Manderston Estate and can be looked at separately; these include the house, the policies and estate farm. As described above the house has undergone several rebuilds and enlargements from the original 18$^{th}$ century mansion house. Today's building has a main two storey (plus basement and attic) block with a slightly lower bachelors wing and U-plan service court with a motor court. There is an elegant interior to both the main house and the servants range, the latter of a far higher standard than was normal for the period. To the rear and sides of the house is a series of formal terraces. The terrace to the south of the house is the oldest, constructed c.1890, overlooks the artificial lake and contains statuary and two small ponds. The terraces to the east of the house comprise a croquet lawn with raised viewing area and a tennis court and are completed by an ornamental doocot or garden house in the north-east corner.

To the north of the main block are the formal kitchen gardens which are enclosed by a high stone wall and entered through an impressive set of gates. Within the walls the garden is divided into different sections including a Fountain Garden and Sunken Garden and to the rear is a set of greenhouses and a fernery. These gardens provided a range of fruit, vegetables and flowers for the estate. To the north and east of the walled gardens are two courts of buildings, one a range of domestic dwellings for the head gardener, estate workers and engineer and the other a farm court, incorporating the dairy.

The oldest of these buildings is the set of cottages which comprise the majority of the "residential" court. These cottages date from the early 18$^{th}$ century and are similar to rows of farm workers cottages throughout the Borders. In the south-west corner is an ornate Head Gardener's cottage, built in the Scottish Renaissance style in 1897 to imitate Argyll's Lodging at Stirling and abutted to the west by lean-to implement sheds. Completing this block is an Engineer's House which adjoins the court on its north-east angle. This two storey building, also built in 1897 to emulate earlier 17$^{th}$ century designs, was home to the engineer in charge of maintaining the estate machinery (located nearby).

The other court comprises a variety of buildings such as are found on farms throughout the Borders. This quadrangular court is abutted to the south by a dairy court and a bullock court on the north-east. The court is entered from the north through a round arch and beside this is a two storey granary which is accessed via a stone stair to the first floor level. Single storey cattle sheds take up the western range of this courtyard and the eastern by haylofts, stable compartments and storage. The owners indulged in many elaborate embellishments, and a decorative turreted tower enhances even the so-called Bullock Court on the north-east side, although it is a fully functional farm building. The dairy range on the south, complete with dairyman's house and a "dairy tower" is spectacularly appointed. Set on the east side of a small dairy court are a dairy *byre*, a boiler house and a dairy scullery. The interior is finished off with several colours of marble and a vaulted ceiling terminating in a carved *boss* depicting a cow and a milkmaid. Adjoining the dairy is an ornate tower approached by an external stone staircase flanked by unicorns. The interior contained an ornate milk house in the form of a monastic chapter house and a tea room. On the other side of the courtyard is the dairyman's house which is as elegantly designed as the rest of the range.

A stable block situated to the west of the walled gardens completes the group. This was home to the owner's thoroughbreds and racehorses. This is a beautiful range of buildings located around a cobbled central courtyard which is entered via an arch. Within are a tack room, stalls and loose boxes. The latter include marble panels carved with the names of the horses, all of which began with "M", above each feeding trough.

Although there are many of the features of smaller farms present at Manderston, large estates are not typical of Border farms. Smaller farms had many of the features of the home farm of an estate but would be constructed with greater emphasis on functionality than decoration.

## Industrial remains

Almost all of the larger settlements in the Borders grew as a result of the Industrial Revolution and all of them still retain to a greater or lesser degree the buildings and landscapes that reflect that growth. A good example of the development of an industrial complex from nothing is Walkerburn, which owes its very existence to the textile industry (**Plate 15**). As late as 1771, when John Ainslie produced his map of the County of Selkirk there was no settlement where Walkerburn now stands. The village was founded in or around 1854 as a centre for the textile industry. The focus of the settlement was a large mill known as Tweedvale (Ballantyne's) Mill, located on the south side of the modern A72, by the Walker Burn. The mill was founded in 1855 and comprises a complex of buildings, the oldest of which is a four storey block with a castellated clock tower. This dominates the rest of the complex, which is mainly made up of two storey buildings. Attached to the engine house of the mill is a fine octagonal brick chimney with a flared top. The mill was powered by a lade from the Walker Burn which passed through Alexandra Park and entered the Tweed behind the modern Tweedholm Avenue East. Immediately to the north of the village, a pair of mill ponds was used to regulate the water flow from the burn and one of these still survives. Associated with the new mill were cottages for the workers. New accommodation, named "Tweedvale Cottages", was built to house the mill workers; these were located to the north-west of the mill in the area now known as "High Cottages".

A second factory, Tweedholm Mill (now Tweedvale Mills East), was constructed to the east of Ballantyne's Mill, at the south end of what is now Jubilee Road. This mill was also a textile (woollen) mill and cottages were also built for its workforce. Many of the houses that front onto Galashiels Road (A72) date from the mid-19th century. In addition to accommodation for the workers, the factory owners and managers also had houses custom-built. These houses are almost all set back in gardens on the north side of the A72. The largest of these is Stoneyhill, which was built in 1868, for mill owner John Ballantyne. This impressive building designed in the early French Gothic style, by FT Pilkington, reflected Ballantyne's position in the community. Equally eye-catching is the pair of gate lodges which flank the approach to the house and sit beside the A72. These lozenge plan buildings were designed in "idiosyncratic Ruskinian early Gothic style" and emphasised the wealth and rank of their owner.

In addition to accommodation, other facilities were provided for the growing population. A school was built for the workers' children on the haughland to the west of the mills and this now forms part of Walkerburn Primary School. By the turn of the 19th century, the village had increased in size and "new housing" was built along the Galashiels road and on Hall Street, so named on account of the village hall which still stands by the main road at the north end of the street. To look after the spiritual needs of the community, two churches were built: the Church of Scotland building on the north of the A72, and a Congregational Chapel opposite. Only the Church of Scotland building is now in use as a church, both still survive as evidence of a period when religion played a more important part in the social life of the community. Leisure facilities were limited but a bowling green was formed on the south side of the Tweed near the station and this also still survives today. To ensure law and order prevailed in this growing town, a Police Station was built at the foot of Hall Street (at the junction of what is now Park Avenue and Tweedholm Avenue East). In common with many rural settlements, the Police Station has been closed and, in this particular

# Farm and Factory: Revolution in the Borders

case, converted into a private home. The final feature worth noting with regards to the growth of Walkerburn, is a cast iron urinal, erected in or around 1897 to improve public sanitation. This structure, cast at the Saracen Foundry in Glasgow, is a unique survival in the Borders and was hailed by the Public Inspector of Sanitation *"a great improvement has been effected in Walkerburn Village by the erection of a public urinal"*. The urinal stands beside the main road, by the Walker Burn, and is now a Listed Building.

The development of Walkerburn highlights many features and themes that occurred in other Border towns. The construction of woollen mills was invariably beside a river or lade system and exit points for this system can still be seen at Hawick on the Slitrig a short distance upstream from Tower Mill and at the junction of the Slitrig and the Teviot. In Galashiels parts of the extensive lade system can be seen to the rear of Bank Street Gardens, in Cornmill Square, in Hall Street and at various other locations through the town. The presence of a lade system in a settlement may also be deduced from the location of mills. In Hawick, mills in the Commercial Road and Mansfield areas were fed by an extensive lade which originally took its water from a cauld on the Teviot at the entrance to Wilton Lodge Park (**fig.27**). Although many of these mills are no longer functioning, they still stand in these areas and are integral parts of the landscape of the Teviot. In Innerleithen an extensive lade which was fed from a cauld on the Leithen Water (near the present golf course) powered not only woollen mills, but also sawmills, an engineering works and Robert Smail's Print Works.

Similarly, it is possible to trace the development of many settlements through the housing built both for the workers and for the factory owners. Workers' houses were distinctive, built in long terraced rows of two or three storeys, often divided into flats, as can be seen on Buckholmside (Galashiels) or beside the Teviot in the Duke Street area of Hawick. The homes of the mill owners were invariably larger and

***Fig.27*** *Wilton Mills, Hawick. This mid-19th century mill was powered by water from an elaborate series of lades diverted from the River Teviot.*

set back from the town. Examples of this type of dwelling may be seen in the Orchard Terrace area of Hawick and along Abbotsford Road in Galashiels. As in Walkerburn, other buildings, constructed for a variety of purposes were also built, including schools, poorhouses and libraries (or reading rooms). Although many of these buildings have been demolished or converted to other uses, some still remain within the townscapes. In Kelso, for instance, the former "Ragged School", survives in Roxburgh Street as a private house, while in Galashiels, St Peter's Episcopal School on Abbotsford Road, (built 1859) now houses the Galashiels office of Scottish Borders Council's Lifelong Care Section.

## *Manufacturing*

The vast majority of the industrial remains within the Borders are connected with the textile industry. However, many smaller manufacturing industries also existed such as corn mills, smithies, joineries, breweries and brick works. Although many of these industries and the buildings associated with them have now vanished, some examples of this piece of the Borders heritage still exist.

The designed villages of Carlops, Denholm (Cavers), and Newcastleton were created to act as stimuli to the improvement of the weaving industry. Each village specialised in a different kind of weaving and each has its own unique features. The present layout of these villages dates to the end of the 18th century, although both Denholm and Carlops may have been small settlements prior to their development.

The largest of the three is Newcastleton, which was founded in 1793 by the third Duke of Buccleuch as a handloom weaving village. The original village consisted of the main street and another parallel to it. The main street had a little square at either end (North and South Hermitage Square) and a larger square in the centre (Douglas Square). The parallel street (North and South Liddel Street) was beside the Liddel Water and had houses on one side only facing the river. No. 44 North Hermitage Street is credited as being the first completed house and bears a date stone of 1793 with initials of the first occupant, Francis Ballantine, above the door. There were 220 houses in the village by 1800, each built at a cost of between £20 and £40. The houses were generally a single storey, with slate roofs and a large front window to provide light for the loom. Although the village has grown, it retains much of its original layout and character.

The village of Denholm was a small hamlet before the 18th century when stocking weavers from Hawick set up businesses there. Several stocking weaving factories were built in the village and housing was also constructed for the weavers around what is now the village green. In the centre of the green is a monument to one of the village's most famous sons, Dr John Leyden. This tall obelisk was erected on the site of the village school, which was removed from the green around 1858. Two of the factories, or stocking-shops as they were known, still exist within the village. The best preserved of these is situated on the west side of the village. It is an oblong building of rubble construction with slate roof. The factory contained three floors and had a dovecot on the roof. Visible on the two upper floors is a regular series of small windows that were each intended to light a stocking machine.

Carlops was created to serve a third type of weaver, that of cotton. The settlement may have had its origins in the Middle Ages but was never a very populous place. In the early 18th century the place was little more than a small mansion house and an inn. However, this changed around 1784, when Robert Brown, the laird of Newhall, began to establish a cotton weaving industry there. The growth of the settlement was rapid and, in 1834, the minister of the parish was able to record that *"formerly six families occupied the site of the village of Carlops, now consisting of 36 houses, and containing 177 inhabitants.*

# Farm and Factory: Revolution in the Borders

**Fig.28** *A 19th century saw mill at Kailzie. Cutting timber was a laborious job for two men with a sawpit before waterpower was harnessed to drive the saws.*

*They are mostly cotton weavers"*. Weavers' cottages were established on either side of the Edinburgh-Biggar turnpike immediately to the south of Carlops Bridge. In 1800, the place was further developed when Alexander Alexander, a weaver from West Linton, set up a water powered woollen mill, using local wool for the supply of felts to the local paper mills. The prosperity of the village was, however, short lived and did not survive the introduction of steam power elsewhere. By the end of the 19th century it was little more than a quiet summer health resort, which enjoyed some prosperity on account of its associations with the poet Allan Ramsay.

Although there have been alterations and additions much of the village retains its original character. Features of note are the rows of 18th century weavers' cottages on either side of the main road, the Allan Ramsay Hotel, Patie's Mill and Carlops Mains. The weavers cottages are of rubble construction augmented with sandstone dressings, and although some were originally pantiled, they now have slate roofs. As built, these cottages accommodated a kitchen and parlour, partitioned off from a central passage which led from the front door to the back of the property. Weaving could have been carried out in either room and there would have been provision for a number of box beds. Behind each cottage was a garden which could be used to grow vegetables and other produce. Set apart from the weavers' cottages, the Allan Ramsay Hotel originated as a wool store, but was converted to use as an inn by the mid-19th century. The farmhouse, Carlops Mains, sits at the south of the village and is said to have originated as an inn. From its architectural design it is certainly contemporary with the rest of the village. The ensemble is rounded off by Patie's Mill, which sits on the North side of the North Esk (Midlothian). It is a well-constructed two-storey structure of rubble and sandstone dressings, bearing an inscribed lintel above the main entrance with the date 1800. This was the woollen mill constructed by Alexander

*Fig.29 Midlem Smiddy. This traditional blacksmith's shop is one of the last working smithies in Scotland.*

Alexander and was later converted to a corn mill after the decline of the textile industry in the village.

Smaller industries had been an important feature of the rural economy from at least as early as the Middle Ages. Almost every village had, at one time, its own smithy and, although less widespread, some communities also had their own sawmill (**fig.28**). Smithies were common, and even tiny hamlets such as Lempitlaw (Kelso) and Edington (Chirnside) possessed one. Their importance was recognised and the blacksmith was often a highly regarded and important member of the community. Indeed, at Ancrum, Midlem (**fig.29**) and Swinton the smithy was situated by the village green, emphasising its central role in the life of the village. Most of these buildings were simple rectangular structures, originally of wood but later replaced in stone to reduce the risk of fire. Dominating one end was a canopied hearth or forge with a *tuyere*, through which the fire was heated by blasts of air from a bellows. It was not unusual for this to be located within a specially designed bellows recess. In the smithies at Nether Horsbrugh (Innerleithen) and Kirkton Manor there were cooling troughs under the forges. Most would also have shuttered windows to cut down on draughts and some would have anvil blocks and a "shoeing room" next door.

## *Rural Industrial Activities*

There are only a few areas of the Borders which possess mineral deposits and consequently the Borders has not been subject to large scale exploitative industries. Quarrying, peat extraction and mining have all taken place to a limited degree, usually to serve the needs of local communities. Some of the earliest large scale quarrying occurred in the 12th century as part of the construction of the Border Abbeys and the large Dingleton Quarry above Melrose continued to be exploited for later building in the town. The amount of quarrying for new buildings, stone dykes and roads increased rapidly in the 18th and 19th centuries. Stone for new field enclosures was often quarried from small pits on site and these old "borrow pits" for dykes and road stone are common features in upland landscapes.

The West Linton area saw quarrying on a relatively large scale. Building stone was extracted from large sandstone quarries at Deepsykehead and many smaller pits. There were large quarries where limestone was extracted and burned for use in the agricultural sector. Several well-preserved lime kilns still survive, most notably at Deepsyke and Bents Quarry. On the floor of the former limestone quarry at Upper Whitfield (now under forestry) the remains of several *clamp kilns* are still visible. The area also saw quarrying or mining for coal, lead and silver which has left a number of scars on the landscape, particularly at Siller Holes where the bell pits for the lead mines still dot the hillside. Around Carlops and on Harlaw Muir there are several examples of redundant coalmines.

The Agricultural Revolution also saw, for the first time, large scale extraction of calcareous marl from many of the marshy hollows of the region for use on arable land. The area around Lindean Reservoir used to be known as Wester Lang Moss and parts of it opened up for marl during the late 18th and early 19th centuries by the lairds of Lindean and Greenhead (both Selkirk). The excavated pits were abandoned after marl extraction ceased and they filled with water to become new lochs and mires. In 1904 the South East of Scotland Water Board constructed a small dam at the eastern end of the largest of these former marl workings and formed a reservoir. This was enlarged in 1936 by raising the height of the dam. Lindean ceased to be used as a public water supply in 1972 and is now utilised as an important local Wildlife Reserve, as well as a fishing and leisure resource.

During the 19th century clean water supplies became an increasingly important requirement for growing towns and cities and suitable rural valleys were examined as possible reservoir sites. Talla reservoir (**Plate 16**) was created by the Edinburgh and District Water Trustees (later the Corporation of Edinburgh), to be the main water supply for the city. The project received parliamentary approval in 1895 and the work was undertaken between 1895 and 1905. Aside from the reservoir itself, many other features still visible in the landscape include a railway, an aqueduct and a series of sighting towers. To bring materials and workers to the site a new length of railway was constructed from Broughton to connect with the Peebles to Biggar line. This branch line took two and a half years to complete and stretches of the track bed still survive beside the modern A701 road. After the work was completed on the railway, construction began on the embankment dam which is made of earth, with a clay wall in the middle and carried into the solid rock. All the construction materials were brought to the site from Carluke (Lanarkshire) via the railway. An overflow carries off surplus water which is channelled along an aqueduct 56km (35 miles) long to Edinburgh. This aqueduct consists, in part, of tunnels through the Tweedsmuir Hills and stone sighting towers built for their alignment can be seen along the route, for example on Nicklebeard and Worm Hills (Tweedsmuir) and Harlaw Muir. The conduit is carried across a number of streams on aqueducts, for example over the Glenmore, Logan (both Tweedsmuir) and Bryland Burn (Kirkurd) and breather vents are a common feature visible along its route.

In the neighbouring Megget Valley is another reservoir, this one of much more recent construction. This is the Megget Reservoir, which was constructed in 1983 as the main drinking water supply serving the Lothian Regions and the city of Edinburgh. The road between Megget and Talla runs among some of the highest hills of the Borders and provides exceptional views of the reservoirs and the wild, upland landscape.

# Farm and Factory: Revolution in the Borders

## Further Reading

**Barry, T & Hall, D 1997**. Spottiswoode: Life and Labour on a Berwickshire Estate, 1753-1793. Tuckwell Press, Phantassie, East Lothian.

**Dent, J & McDonald, R 1997**. Early Settlers in the Borders. Scottish Borders Council, Newtown St Boswells.

**Dent, J & McDonald, R 1998**. Christian Heritage in the Borders. Scottish Borders Council, Newtown St Boswells.

**Dent, J & McDonald, R 2000**. Warfare and Fortifications in the Borders. Scottish Borders Council, Newtown St Boswells.

**Devine, T M & Mitchison, R (eds.) 1988**. People and Society in Scotland, Volume I, 1760-1830. Arrowsmith, Bristol.

**Fraser, W H & Morris, R J (eds.) 2000**. People and Society in Scotland, Volume II, 1830-1914. Arrowsmith, Bristol.

**Haldane, A R B 1997**. The Drove Roads of Scotland. Birlinn Limited, Edinburgh.

**Hume, J R 1976**. The Industrial Archaeology of Scotland: 1. The Lowlands and Borders. Batsford, London.

**Jones, W 1996**. Dictionary of Industrial Archaeology. Sutton Publishing, Stroud.

**Lambert, R A (ed) 1998**. Species History in Scotland. Scottish Cultural Press, Edinburgh.

**Mackay, J J 1998**. Border Highways. John James Mackay, Kelso.

**Robson, M 1989**. An Ingenious Mechanic of Scotland: James Small (c.1740-1793).

**Robson, M 1991**. A Break with the Past: Changed Days on Two Border Sheep Farms.

**Sanderson, M 1982**. Scottish Rural Society in the 16th century. John Donald, Edinburgh.

**Smout, T C 1969**. A History of the Scottish People 1560-1830. Fontana Press, London.

**Smout, T C 2000**. Nature Contested. Edinburgh University Press, Edinburgh.

**Symon, J A 1959**. Scottish Farming Past and Present. Oliver & Boyd, Edinburgh.

**Whyte I 1979**. Agriculture and Society in the 17th century. John Donald, Edinburgh.

**Whyte, I 1990**. Edinburgh & the Borders Landscape Heritage. David & Charles, London.

# Farm and Factory; Revolution in the Borders

# Glossary

**antacid:** a substance which neutralises acids.

**arboretum:** a living museum where trees, shrubs and herbaceous plants are cultivated for scientific and educational purposes.

**bere:** an primitive variety of barley.

**boll:** obsolete measure.

**bonnet laird:** the lowest rank of landowner, equivalent to an English yeoman farmer.

**boss:** an ornamental knob or other projection which covers the intersection of ribs in a ribbed vault.

**byre:** farm building where cattle are kept.

**Cato:** Marcus Porcius Cato (234-149 BC), Roman statesman, orator and writer.

**cauld:** a dam thrown obliquely across a river to raise a head of water and feed a *lade* (q.v.).

**clamp kiln:** a temporary kiln, in which the pots are stacked and baked in a pit beneath a bonfire.

**cruck:** structural support made from a naturally curving tree trunk. Two or three pairs of crucks, in the shape of an inverted 'V', commonly formed the primary supports for the walls and roof of a medieval farmhouse.

**cutwater:** the projecting element of a bridge pier, usually either v-shaped or semicirclar.

**Doric:** the plainest form of classical Greek architectural style.

**dyke:** wall of stone (or turf).

**espalier:** tree or shrub trained to grow on a wall face.

**ferm toun:** "farm town"; a hamlet with a farm as its main focus.

**feudal:** social system, in which the sovereign was the ultimate source of all rights to the use or occupation of land.

**greywacke:** hard, ancient sedimentary rock which comprises much of the Southern Uplands.

**heritor:** the proprietor of heritable property; a landowner.

**hydro-electric:** term applied to power generated by a water-driven turbine.

**igneous:** formed from molten rock (as opposed to water or wind born sediments).

**infield:** arable land immediately adjacent to a pre-enclosure settlement.

**kailyard:** vegetable patch, usually in rural setting.

**kirk toun:** "church town"; a hamlet centred on a church.

**lade:** artificial channel or leet to receive water ponded by a *cauld* (q.v.) and divert it from a river or stream to drive a mill wheel.

**laird:** the landlord of an estate, often equated with the English squire.

**lochan:** small loch or mere.

**mains:** home farm of an estate.

**marl:** lime enriched clay used to reduce the acidity of soil.

**outfield:** sporadically cultivated land located at a distance from a pre-enclosure settlement.

**pantile:** clay roofing tile.

**Reformation:** religious revolution, which in Scotland occurred in 1560 and resulted in multiple approaches to the Christian faith at the expense of Roman Catholicism.

**reiver:** member of frontier society who engaged in kidnapping, rustling, extortion, burglary and/or murder as a way of life.

**Renaissance:** re-emergence of classical culture which ended the monopoly on learning previously held by the medieval church and led to a burgeoning of scientific, artistic and philosophical developments.

**rotary gin:** a geared beam turned by a draught animal to drive early farm machinery. Normally housed in a round or polygonal building next to the threshing barn.

**shiel:** temporary accommodation for salmon fishers.

**shieling:** summer shelter used by herds tending stock on high or remote pastures.

**spinning jenny:** an 18th century hand operated machine capable of spinning several yarns at once.

**spinning mule:** labour saving yarn spinning device which combined the best parts of the *spinning jenny* and *water frame*.

**stead:** a farm.

**tenant-at-will:** tenant who by custom or usage occupies land on which he has spent money (e.g. on buildings) and for which pays ground rent, but without a written lease or acknowledged term of occupancy.

**threshing:** separation of cereal grain from the rest of the plant.

**toun:** "town" in the archaic sense of hamlet or village.

**turnpike:** improved road, the cost of which was recovered from tolls.

**tuyere:** nozzle through which air is forced to increase the heat of a furnace.

**water frame:** a water-powered cotton spinning machine.

**winnowing:** use of wind to separate chaff from seeds.

# Farm and Factory: Revolution in the Borders

# Farm and Factory: Revolution in the Borders

## Sites to Visit

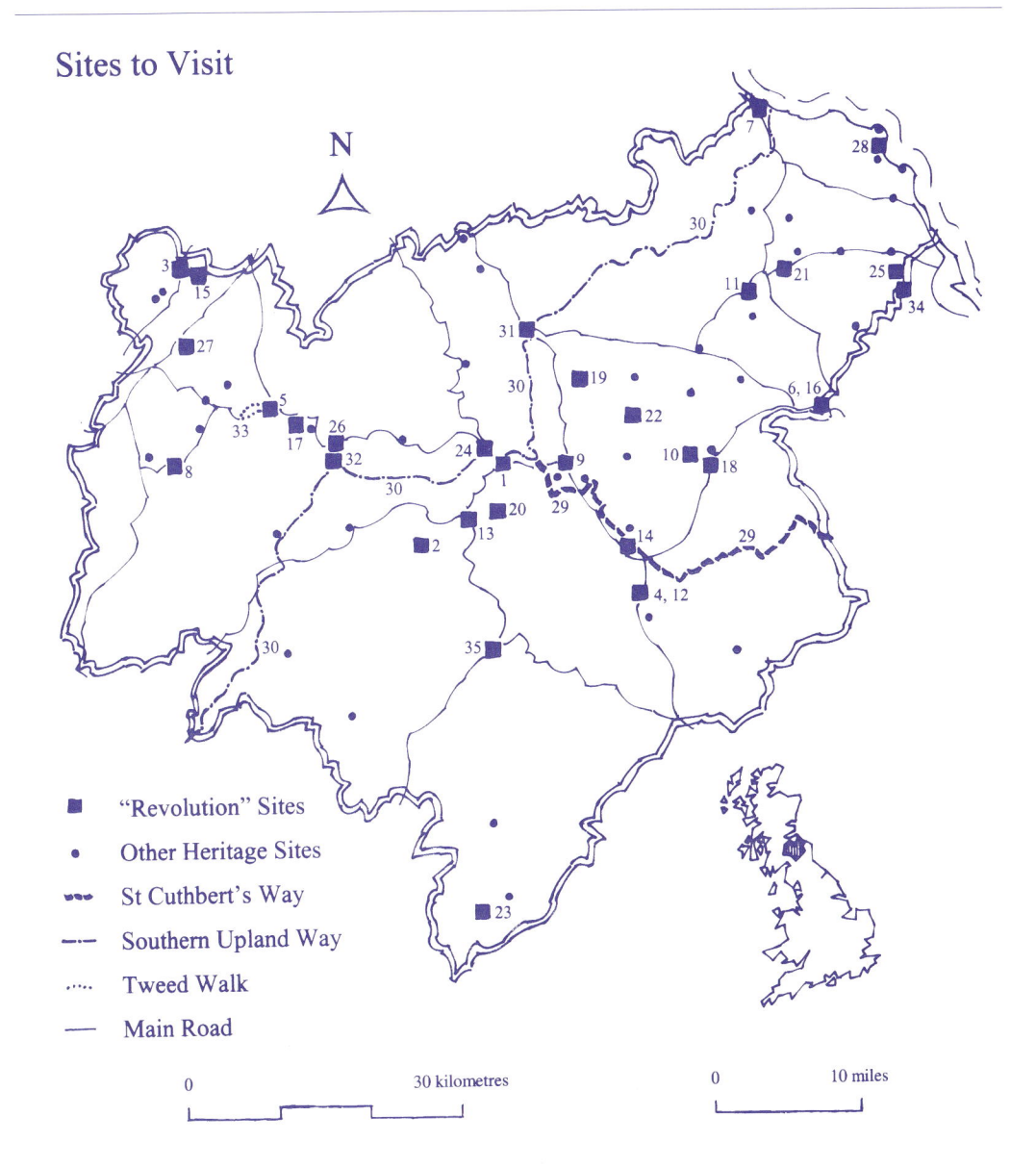

- ■ "Revolution" Sites
- • Other Heritage Sites
- ••• St Cuthbert's Way
- —•— Southern Upland Way
- ..... Tweed Walk
- — Main Road

*Fig.30 Sites to Visit.*

For details of opening times and admission charges please consult your nearest Tourist Information Centre, or contact:

Jedburgh Tourist Information Centre
Murray's Green
Jedburgh
Roxburghshire
TD8 6BE

In addition to these Sites to Visit, Duns, Eyemouth, Galashiels, Hawick, Jedburgh, Lauder, Peebles and Selkirk have numerous monuments of the Industrial Revolution in the Borders. Town Trails provide further information about the development of these settlements.

*Farm and Factory: Revolution in the Borders*

### 1  Abbotsford House, Melrose; NT 508 342

Home of the author Sir Walter Scott. Abbotsford was built between 1817-24 and is situated within a designed landscape, which was laid out by the author. Open to the public. Admission Charge.

### 2  Aikwood Tower, James Hogg Exhibition; NT 420 260

This tower house was home to the Scotts of Aikwood and was built in the closing years of the old frontier. The recently restored tower was a familiar landmark to the poet and writer, James Hogg, the "Ettrick Shepherd", who is the subject of an exhibition in the adjoining byre. Open Seasonally. Admission Charge.

### 3  Carlops, West Linton; NT 160 560

The existing village of Carlops was founded in 1784 when Robert Brown, laird of Newhall, began to establish a cotton-weaving industry. In 1800 a West Linton weaver, Alexander Alexander, set up a water-powered woollen mill in the village, using coarse Tweeddale wool. This prosperity was short-lived, and by the end of the 19$^{th}$ century it was little more than a summer health-resort, enjoying some renown on account of its associations with the poet Allan Ramsay.

### 4  Castle Jail & Museum, Castlegate, Jedburgh;  NT 647 201

The Victorian prison, now a museum of local history, is situated on the site of the Royal Castle of Jedburgh and contains various exhibits relating to the history and development of the town and surrounding area. Admission Charge.

### 5  Chambers Institute, High Street, Peebles; NT 253 403

William "Dictionary" Chambers was a native of Peebles and gave 'Queensberry Lodging' or 'Dean's House' to the town for the purposes of 'social improvement'. Today it houses the local museum, which hosts regular exhibitions about the history and culture of the Borders.

### 6  Coldstream Museum, Market Place, Coldstream; NT 843 397

A local history museum, which includes exhibits on the lifestyles of inhabitants of the area in the 18$^{th}$ and 19$^{th}$ centuries.

### 7  Cove Harbour, Cockburnspath; NT 784 717

The breakwaters were completed in 1831 and consist of two piers, on the north and south, forming a simple harbour. **The harbour is in private ownership and is visible from the Southern Upland Way (30).**

### 8  Dawyck Botanical Gardens, Drumelzier; NT 167 351

Dawyck is home to a fine collection of historic conifers, many of which are outstanding examples of their kind. In addition to its wealth of North American species, it boasts unusual Asiatic Chinese trees, and is the source of the Dawyck Beech. There is also a wide range of flowering shrubs. Open Seasonally. Admission Charge.

## 9  Drygrange Bridge & Leaderfoot Viaduct, Melrose; NT 575 346

Three bridges representing different developments in the transport network of the Borders can be seen from this viewpoint and are interpreted in the work of a local artist. They are a turnpike bridge, railway viaduct and a modern road bridge. **There is no public access to the Leaderfoot Viaduct.**

## 10  Floors Castle, Kelso; NT 711 346

To the north of Kelso and within easy walking distance of the Town Square is Floors Castle (reputedly the largest house in Scotland). It was designed and built for the first Duke of Roxburghe by William Adam between 1721-6. The house was extensively remodelled between 1837-45 by William H Playfair to give it its present imposing appearance. The house is privately owned by the present Duke of Roxburghe but is open to the public. Admission Charge.

## 11  Gavinton Planned Village, Langton; NT 768 521

David Gavin, laird of Langton Estate, built Gavinton in the latter half of the 18$^{th}$ century. His purpose was to landscape the surroundings of his home and provide his tenants with a modern settlement in which to pursue their cottage industries.

## 12  Greyfriars Garden, Jedburgh; NT 650 208

The foundations of the last monastic house to be founded in Scotland are visible in this garden. Many medicinal herbs and local varieties of fruit tree are to be seen here, and interpretation tells the story of the 16$^{th}$ century house of Observantine Franciscan friars and its destruction at the hands of English gunners in 1545.

## 13  Halliwell's House Museum, Selkirk; NT 469 284

The museum describes the history of Selkirk and its development to modern times. Interesting exhibits include relics of the Turnpike Era.

## 14  Harestanes Countryside Visitor Centre, Ancrum; NT 641 244

Harestanes Countryside Visitor Centre provides interpretation on local wildlife as well as the opportunity to walk in the designed landscape of Monteviot House. Harestanes was originally the Home farm for Monteviot Estate and the buildings are good examples of how a 19$^{th}$ century farm would have been laid out. Harestanes is also situated close to St Cuthbert's Way **(29)** and the Dere Street Walk. Open April to October.

## 15  Harlaw Muir, West Linton; NT 180 546

On the north-west side of the road through Harlaw Muir is a square stone tower that once served as a siting tower during the construction of the Talla mains water supply from the new reservoir to Edinburgh. **There is no access to the tower which should only be viewed from the outside.**

## 16  The Hirsel, Coldstream; NT 827 402

Situated 3.5km (2 miles) north-west of Coldstream, this estate has been the seat of the Earls of Home since the early 17$^{th}$ century. The 14$^{th}$ Earl, as Sir Alec Douglas-Home, was Prime Minister from 1963 to 1964. The estate is open daily and includes an exhibit on rural life on the estate, nature trails, the Hirsel Lake (a wildfowl sanctuary), and Dundock Wood, notable for its rhododendrons and azaleas. Open daily. Admission Charge.

## *Farm and Factory; Revolution in the Borders*

### 17  Kailzie Gardens, Traquair; NT 281 385

Designed landscape of former Kailzie House (demolished 1962). Within the walled garden are greenhouses, herbaceous borders, many unusual species of shrubs, laburnum arches and a rose garden. Near the site of the old house is the a dovecot and duckpond. Other attractions include an Art Gallery, Gift Shop, Tearoom and Licensed Restaurant and the Children's Corner. Admission Charge.

### 18  Kelso Bridge; NT 727 336

The elegant five span bridge which crosses the River Tweed at the entrance to the medieval burgh of Kelso was designed by John Rennie and constructed between 1800-03. This bridge replaces an earlier one which had been swept away during a flood in 1797. At the eastern end of the bridge is a tollhouse of the same date.

### 19  Legerwood Farm Trail; NT 586 433

Situated in the midst of Lauderdale, Legerwood Farm lies midway between the sheep farms of the Southern Uplands (to the west) and the lower fertile arable farms of the Merse (to the east). It is a typical farm of this area and mixes livestock with arable. The farm trail is open to the public and there is a leaflet highlighting the many interesting features of such a farm.

### 20  Lindean Reservoir, Nr Selkirk; NT 503 291

Lindean Reservoir was formed in 1904 from former marl workings. No longer an active reservoir, Lindean is home to a variety of plant, animal, bird and insect species including water plantain (spectacular in May when it flowers), the Reed Bunting and Little Grebe.

### 21  Manderston House, Duns; NT 810 543

Although the original house dates to the 1790s much of what can be seen by the visitor belongs to the late $19^{th}$ and early $20^{th}$ centuries, when John Kinross extensively redesigned Manderston, on behalf of the Miller family. The Millers had made their fortune trading hemp and herring with Russia and spared no expense in refurbishing their new home. Open seasonally. Admission Charge.

### 22  Mellerstain House, Earlston; NT 647 390

Mellerstain House, the home of the Earl and Countess of Haddington, is one of Scotland's finest Georgian mansions. Designed by William and Robert Adam it is famous for its ceilings, superb collection of paintings and fine period furniture. A designed landscape that includes parkland, a lake and gardens with attractive parterres and terraces surrounds the house. Open seasonally (closed on Saturdays). Admission Charge.

### 23  Newcastleton; NY 483 874

The parish of Castleton consisted in the $18^{th}$ century of a series of scattered farms which in 1793 were reorganised by the third Duke of Buccleuch into the planned village of Newcastleton. A small museum run by the Liddesdale Heritage Association provides additional information about the area.

## Farm and Factory: Revolution in the Borders

### 24 Old Gala House, Galashiels; NT 491 358

Originally a tower house built by the Pringles of Gala in the late 16th century. This building has been modified and extended on several occasions and now serves as the local museum and art gallery. A nearby park known as Gala Policies represents the remaining portion of a designed landscape, within which old Gala House and its successor (now demolished) stood.

### 25 Paxton House, Hutton; NT 931 519

Built in 1758 for Patrick Home of Billie on the bank of the River Tweed, Paxton is one of the finest 18th century Palladian country houses in Britain. It boasts interiors by Robert Adam, furniture by Thomas Chippendale, and the largest picture gallery in a Scottish Country House. Paxton is one of the National Galleries of Scotland and houses over 70 paintings from the national collections. The gardens are also open to the public. Open Seasonally. Admission Charge.

### 26 Robert Smail's Print Works, Innerleithen; NT 332 367

A completely restored printing works. The buildings contain an office, paper store with reconstructed water wheel, composing and pressrooms. Visitors can discover the secrets of the printing works from archive-based posters, by watching the printer at work and by trying type-setting by hand. Many historic items and photographs on display also give a fascinating insight into this small Borders town. Open seasonally. Admission Charge.

### 27 Romannobridge, Cultivation Terraces; NT 162 470

On the south west slopes of Penria Hill, near Romannobridge are a very well preserved set of cultivation terraces. They are best viewed from the A701 between Mountain Cross and Romannobridge. **Please note there is no public access to this site.**

### 28 St Abbs, Village & Harbour; NT 919 672

St Abbs is a picturesque fishing village situated a few miles north of Eyemouth. The village came into existence during the 19th century with the creation of a harbour in 1831 as a refuge for fishing-boats. Much of the old harbour still survives and has changed very little from the original design.

### 29 St Cuthbert's Way

A 100 kilometre (62 mile) long distance footpath from Melrose to Lindisfarne. The route passes close by to the Temple of the Muses, Mertoun Bridge and Harestanes Countryside Visitor Centre **(14)**.

### 30 Southern Upland Way

A 340 kilometre (212 mile) long distance coast to coast footpath from Portpatrick on the west to Cockburnspath on the east. The path passes close to Abbotsford House **(1)**, Cove Harbour **(7)**, Thirlestane Castle **(31)**. Old Gala House **(24)**, Robert Smail's Print Works **(26)** and Traquair House **(32)**. Further details available from Tourist Information Centres.

## 31 Thirlestane Castle, Lauder; NT 533 479

A magnificent late 16th century castle built under the direction of John Maitland, Chancellor of Scotland. The building was enlarged in the 1670s and adorned with some particularly fine plaster ceilings, commissioned by the 1st Earl of Lauderdale. The castle and its policies, or parkland were laid out over the remains of an earlier fortification occupied by King Edward II in 1324 and subsequently converted into an English artillery fort in 1548. Admission Charge.

## 32 Traquair House; NT 330 354

A 15th century tower house, which was extended into a comfortable 16th and 17th century mansion and retains much of its historic character. Traquair sits within its own designed landscape, which includes a river diversion to move the Tweed away from its walls. The estate brewery is still in operation and is a survival from times when beer was drunk in place of water. Admission Charge.

## 33 Tweed Walk, Peebles

Walkway along the Tweed to Lyne Station which affords access to Neidpath Viaduct. This railway bridge is one of the finest examples of skewed arch construction in Scotland. The viaduct was opened on the 1st February 1864, for the Symington, Biggar & Broughton Railway, which was subsequently taken over by the Caledonian Railway.

## 34 Union Suspension Bridge, Hutton; NT 933 510

Built by Capt. Sir Samuel Brown, with advice from John Rennie in 1819-20, this was the first large suspension bridge in Britain. At each end of the bridge is a large pink sandstone pylon adorned with a plaque bearing by the motto "VIS UNITA FORTIOR 1820", or "stronger united". On the Scottish side of the Tweed stood the Union Bridge Tollhouse which has now been converted into a private dwelling.

## 35 Wilton Lodge Museum, Hawick; NT 493 145

Set within 43 hectares (107 acres) of parkland is Wilton Lodge Museum. The building originated as Langlands House but has been a local history museum since 1910. The museum contains archaeological, local history and zoological collections, which pay particular attention to Hawick district and Teviotdale.

# Index

Abbotsford, 30, 55
Adam, James, 63
Adam, William, 51-52
Ainslie, John, **31**, 69
Alemoor, 56
Alexander, Alexander, 72-73
Ancrum, 73
Ancrum (Bridge), *see Bridges*
Apple, *see Flora*
Apricot, *see Flora*
Argus, Northern Brown, 53
Argyll's Lodging, 68
Argyll, third Duke of, *see Landowners*
Arkwright, Richard, *see Innovators*
Armstrong, Sir William, *see Innovators*
Ashiestiel Bridge, *see Bridges*
Ayton, 40

Ballantyne, John, 69
Ballantyne's Mill, 69, **back cover**
Balsam, Himalayan, *see Flora*
Barley, *see Flora*
Bents Quarry, 74
Bere, *see Flora*
Berwick, 13, 21, 34, 36, 40, 41, 41, 42, 43, 60
Biggar, 55, 72, 74
Billie Mire, 16
Birgham, 37
Birkenside, 59
Bittern, *see Fauna*
Blackadder Mount, 16, 64, 65
Black Barony, 33
Blairbog, 47
Bonnie Prince Charlie, 17
Bowhill, 15, 30
Bowshank, **front cover**
Braemar Knowe, 46
Branxholm, 49

## Bridges
    Ancrum, 21, 36, 60

Ashiestiel, 38
Berwick, 38, 58
Canongate, **37**, 38
Coldstream, 21, 38, 39, 40, 59, 60, **Plate 4**
Drygrange, 39, 60
Dunglass Viaduct, 40, 62
Gattonside Suspension, 39
Kalemouth Suspension, 39
Kelso, 21, 38, 39, **59**
Leaderfoot (Road), 39, 60
Leaderfoot Viaduct, 60, 62
Lowood (Bottle), 60
Mertoun, 39, 60
Neidpath Viaduct, 62
Pease, 59
Roxburgh Viaduct, 38-39, 62, **Plate 13**
Royal Border, 40, 59
Royal Tweed, 59
Shankend Viaduct, 62
Tay, 58
Tweed (Galashiels), 39, 62
Tweed (Peebles), 37, 58
Union Suspension, 21, **38**, 60
Waterloo, 38
Yair, 60

Brieryhill, 55
Brodie, Alexander, 17, 29
Broomdykes, 55
Brown, Capt. Sir Samuel, *see Innovators*
Brown, Robert, *see Landowners*
Bryland Burn, 74
Buccleuch, Duke of, *see Landowners*
Burnmouth, 21, 39, 41, 42, 43, 44, 62
Buxley, *see Manderston*

Caerlee Mill, 17
Carham, 37
Carlisle, 21, 40, 41
Carlops, 17, 18, 53, 71-73
Carluke, 74
Carrot, *see Flora*

## Farm and Factory: Revolution in the Borders

Carter Bar, 59
Cavers, 16
Chicken, *see Fauna*
Chirnside, 15, 30
Chisholme, James, 28
Clarabad, 55
Cleikemin, *see Ancrum Bridge*
Clovenfords, 35
Clover, Red, *see Flora*
Cockburn, Sir Alexander, *see Landowners*
Cockburn, John (of Ormiston), *see Landowners*
Cockburnspath, 33, 39, 40
Coldingham Moor, 39
Coldingham Priory, 21, 33, 34
Coldstream Bridge, *see Bridges*
Cothill, 15
Cove Harbour, 21, 43, 62, **Plate 14**
Cow, *see Fauna*
Cowbog, 16
Cowdenknowes, 25
Craighouse Quarry, 19, 53
Crompton, Samuel, *see Innovators*
Currant, *see Flora*

David I (King of Scotland), 12
Deepsyke Quarry, 74
Deepsykehead Quarry, **48**, 74
Denholm, 71
Dere Street, 58
Dickson, James, **22**
Dingleton Quarry, 73
Dirrington Laws, 46
Dolphinton, 41
Dryburgh Abbey, 34
Drygrange Bridge, *see Bridges*
Duck, *see Fauna*
Dunbar, 36, 40
Dunglass Burn, 40, 42
Dunglass Viaduct, *see Bridges*
Duns, 30, 39, 41, 55, 66

Earlston, 32
East Linton, 16

Easter Mountbenger, 13
Eccles (Parish), 29
Eccles (Priory), 34
Eckford, 33
Eddleston, 41
Edinburgh, 21, 32, 34, 36, 39, 40, 41, 56, 58, 60, **61**, 72, 74
Edington, 73
Ednam House Hotel, **22**
Edrom Newton, 65
Elba, 53
Eucalyptus, *see Flora*
Eyemouth, 21, 34-35, 41, 42-44, **61**, 62, 63

Fast Castle, 44

### Fauna

Bittern, 34
Chicken, 34, 35
Cow, 27, 52, 66
Crab, 43
Duck, 34
Gannet, 34
Goose, 34, 35
Haddock, 43
Hare, 33
Heron, 34
Herring, 34-35, 36, 43, 44
Kittiwake, 34
Lobster, 35, 43
Partridge, 34,
Pheasant, 34
Pigeon, 34, 35
Rabbit, 33, 35, 46
Salmon, 34
Sheep, 14, 28, 33, 36, **47**, **50**, 52
Squirrel, Grey, 52
Squirrel, Red, 52
Skate, 35
Swan, 34
Turkey, 34

Ferniehirst, 25
Fig, *see Flora*

Fir, Douglas, *see Flora*
Flax, *see Flora*
Floors, 15, 25, 35, 66

## Flora
    Apple, 35
    Apricot, 35
    Balsam, Himalayan, **52**
    Barley, 49
    Bere, 35, 49
    Carrot, 35
    Clover, Red, 49
    Currant, 35
    Eucalyptus, 52
    Fig, 35
    Fir, Douglas, 52
    Flax, 49
    Gooseberry, 52
    Hogweed, Giant, 52
    Oats, 13, 49
    Knotweed, Japanese, 52
    Melon, 35
    Monkey-Puzzle, 52
    Pea, 49
    Peach, 35
    Pear, 35
    Pine, Wellingtonia, 52
    Plum, 35
    Potato, 15, 35, 49, 50
    Rhododendron, 52
    Rhubarb, 35
    Rockrose, Common, 53
    Spruce, Sitka, 52
    Turnip, 15, 33, 35, 43, 49, 50, 66
Flowmossmuir, 47
Fountainhall, 41
Fruid, 56

Galashiels, 13, 17, **18**, 25, 28, 29, 30, 32, 34, 41, 54, 55, 60, 69, 70-71
Galashiels (Station), 62
Galashiels (Tweed Bridge), *see Bridges*
Gannet, *see Fauna*

Gattonside, 35, 58
Gavin, David, *see Landowners*
Gavinton, 17, 18, 49, 52
Glasgow, 21, 36, 40, 41, 70
Glengaber Burn, 53
Glenmore Burn, 74
Goose, *see Fauna*
Gooseberry, *see Fauna*
Gordon Moss, 46
Grantshouse, 39, 40
Great North Road, 39, 58
Greenbank Toll, 39, 59
Greenhead, 74
Greenlawdean, 19
Greenlaw Moss, 16
Greenriver, 28
Gretna Green, 40
Gunsgreen House, 63, **Plate 9**
Gunsgreenhill Windmill, 55
Gutcher's Hole, 42

Haddock, *see Fauna*
Hare, *see Fauna*
Hargreaves, James, *see Innovators*
Harlaw Muir, 19, 53, 74
Harmony Hall, 22, 28
Hawick, **18**, 24, 29, **30**, 32, 41, 54, 55, 62, **70** - 71
Hawick (Wilton Park), 35, 70
Heron, *see Fauna*
Herring, *see Fauna*
Herring Road, 35, 36
Hobsburn House, 28
Home, Grisell, Countess of Marchmont, *see Landowners*
Home, Patrick, Earl of Marchmont, *see Landowners*
Hogweed, Giant, *see Flora*
Huttonhall, 25

## Innovators
    Arkwright, Richard, 17, 28
    Armstrong, Sir William, 56
    Brown, Capt. Sir Samuel, 21, 38, 60
    Crompton, Samuel, 17, 28

Hargreaves, James, 28
Jenner, Dr Edward, 29
Macadam, John, 21
Meikle, Andrew, 16
Rennie, John, 21, 38, **59**, 60
Roger, Andrew, 16
Small, James, **16**, **31**
Smeaton, James, 21, 38
Smeaton, John, 63
Telford, Thomas, 21, 40
Watt, James, 28
Innerleithen, 29, **53**, 56, 70
Innerleithen (Station), 62

James VI/I (King of Scotland/England), 25, 38
Jedburgh, 12, 29, 32, 35, 41, 60
Jedburgh, (Canongate Bridge), *see Bridges*
Jedburgh (Greyfriars Garden), 35, **Plate 7**
Jenner, Dr Edward, *see Innovators*

Kailzie, **72**
Kalemouth Suspension Bridge, *see Bridges*
Kames, Lord, *see Landowners*
Kelso, 21, 25, 30, 32, 34, 38, 39, 41, 71
Kelso (Abbey), 25, 35
Kelso (Bridge), *see Bridges*
Ker (of Cessford), *see Landowners*
Ker, Robert, Earl of Ancrum, *see Landowners*
Kerr, John, first Duke of Roxburghe, *see Landowners*
Kimmerghame, 33
Kinross, John, 66
Kirkhope Law, 37
Kirkton Manor, 13, 73
Kirndean Farm, 53
Kirnie Law, 56
Kittiwake, *see Fauna*
Knotweed, Japanese, *see Flora*

Laidlawstiel, 64
Ladykirk, 39, 65
Lamberton Moor, 39, **Plate 8**
Lamberton Toll, 40
Lambertonshiels, 13

## Landowners

Argyll, third Duke of, 14, 47
Brown, Robert, 71
Buccleuch, Duke of, 41, 71
Cockburn, Sir Alexander, 14
Cockburn, John (of Ormiston), 15
Gavin, David, 49, 50, 52
Home, Grisell, Countess of Marchmont, 35
Home, Patrick, Earl of Marchmont, 35
Kames, Lord, 15, 50
Ker (of Cessford), 25
Ker, Robert, Earl of Ancrum, 25
Kerr, John, first Duke of Roxburghe, 15
Maitland, General, 66
Marchmont, Lord, 50
Miller, Sir James, 66
Miller, Robert, 66
Miller, Sir William, 66
Nisbet, Sir Alexander, **26**
Pringle (of Galashiels), 25, 28, 37
Pringle (of Torwoodlee), 25
Rutherford, Dr John, 15
Scott, Sir Walter, 55
Spottiswoode, John, 49
Stair, Lord, 15
Swinton, John, 14
Langton, 15, 49, 52
Larriston, 53
Lauder, 35, 39, 41
Leaderfoot (Road), *see Bridges*
Leaderfoot Viaduct, *see Bridges*
Learmonth, John, 40
Leitholm, **51**
Lempitlaw, 73
Leslie, John, 65
Lessudden House, 25
Lethem, 46, **Plate 10**
Leyden, Dr John, 71
Lilliesleaf, 15, 26, 27, 28, 56
Lindean, 74
Lindean Reservoir, 48, 56, 74, **Plate 11**
Linthill, 35

Lobster, *see Fauna*
Logan Burn, 74
London, 21, 34, 37, 38, 55, 58
London, (Waterloo Bridge), *see Bridges*
Lowood, 37
Lowood (Bottle Bridge), *see Bridges*
Lugate, **65**-66

Macadam, John, *see Innovators*
Maitland, General, *see Landowners*
Malcolm IV (King of Scotland), 33
Manderston, 35, 66-68
Marchmont, 19, 30, 33, 51
Marchmont, Lord, *see Landowners*
Megget, 56, 74
Meikle, Andrew, *see Innovators*
Meldon Burn, 56
Mellerstain, 15, 34, 51, 66, **Plate 12**
Melon, *see Flora*
Melrose, 15, 28, 32, 35, 58, 62, 74
Melrose (Abbey), 32, 54
Melrose (Golf Course), 47
Melrose (Priorwood Gardens), 35
Melrose (Station), **42**, 62
Mertoun (Bridge), *see Bridges*
Mertoun (House), 25
Middlestots Bog, 48
Midlem, 15, 56, **73**, **Plate 1**
Miller, Sir James, *see Landowners*
Miller, Robert, *see Landowners*
Miller, Sir William, *see Landowners*
Monteviot House, **Plate 2**
Monkey-Puzzle, *see Flora*
Mordington, 53
Morow, John, 32

Neidpath Viaduct, *see Bridges*
Nether Horsbrugh, 73
Newcastle, 21, **61**
Newcastleton, 17, 18, 46, 49, 71, **Plate 3**
Newstead, 41, 52
Newton Don, 65
Newtown St Boswells, 56

Nicklebread Hill, 74
Ninewar, 55
Ninewells, **Plate 6**
Nisbet, Sir Alexander, *see Landowners*
Nisbet House, 25-**26**
Nisbet, James, **22**, 63

Oats, *see Flora*
Old Kirkhope, 13
Outer Cock Law, 36
Oxnam, 33, 53

Park, Mungo, **31**, 52
Partridge, *see Fauna*
Patie's Mill, 72
Paxton, 34
Pea, *see Flora*
Peach, *see Flora*
Pear, *see Flora*
Pease Bridge, *see Bridges*
Peebles, 12, 13, 25, 30, 32, 37, 38, 41, 56, 58, 62, 74
Peebles (Tweed Bridge), *see Bridges*
Pheasant, *see Fauna*
Pigeon, *see Fauna*
Pilkington, F T, 69
Pine, Wellingtonia, *see Flora*
Pirn House, 25
Pont, Timothy, 46, 53, 54, 66
Potato, *see Flora*
Plum, *see Flora*
Pringle (of Galashiels), *see Landowners*
Pringle (of Torwoodlee), *see Landowners*

Ramsay, Allan, 72
Redbraes Castle, 26
Redheugh, 44
Rennie, John, *see Innovators*
Rhododendron, *see Flora*
Rhubarb, *see Flora*
Riccarton Junction, 41, 62
Robert's Linn, 53
Rockrose, Common, *see Flora*
Roger, Andrew, *see Innovators*

## Farm and Factory: Revolution in the Borders

Romannobridge, 37, 47
Roxburgh (Old), 13, 37, 38
Roxburgh (Station), 62
Roxburgh (Viaduct), *see Bridges*
Roy, General, 65
Royal Border, *see Bridges*
Royal Tweed, *see Bridges*
Rutherford, Dr John, *see Landowners*

St Abbs, 21, 43, 62, 63
St Boswells, **54**, 56, 62
St Mary's Loch, 51
Salmon, *see Fauna*
Scott, Sir Walter, *see Landowners*
Selkirk, 17, 25, 41, 54, 55, 60
Shankend Viaduct, *see Bridges*
Sheep, *see Fauna*
Sibbald, Sir Robert, 35
Siller Holes, 53, 74
Simprim, 14
Skate, *see Fauna*
Smail, Robert, 70
Smailholm Tower, 64
Small, John, *see Innovators*
Smeaton, James, *see Innovators*
Smeaton, John, *see Innovators*
Soutra, 55
Spittal-on-Rule, 39
Spottiswoode, John, *see Landowners*
Springwood Park, 26
Spruce, Sitka, *see Flora*
Squirrel, Grey, *see Fauna*
Squirrel, Red, *see Fauna*
Stair, Lord, *see Landowners*
Stevenson, David, 63
Stevenson, Thomas, 63
Stobo, 62
Stow, 34
Swan, *see Fauna*
Swinton, John, *see Landowners*
Sundhope, 13

Talla, 56, 74, **Plate 16**

Thieves' Road, 36
Thomas, Telford, *see Innovators*
Thornylee, 39
Threepwood Moss, 46
Torwoodlee Tower, 26
Tower Mill, 70
Traquair, 25
Turkey, *see Fauna*
Turnip, *see Flora*
Tweedholm Mill, 69

Union Suspension Bridge, *see Bridges*

Victoria (Queen of Great Britain), 21
Vitruvius, 54

Walkerburn, 29, 32, 39, 56, 69-71, **Plate 15**
Watt, James, *see Innovators*
Waugh, Robert, 22, 30
Weatherstone, Dalhousie, 66
Webster, Dr Alexander, **24**
Wedderburn, 49
Wester Lang Moss, 48, 74
Wester Mountbenger, 13
West Linton, 19, 48, 52, 53, 72, 74
Whim (Estate), 14
Whim (Moss), 46
Whitrig Bog, **19**, 54
Whitrope Tunnel, 41, 62
Wood, John, 54
Worm Hill, 74

Yair Bridge, *see Bridges*
Yetholm Loch, 16